Longman

# Vocabulary
# MENTOR
# JOY
## 3

 Pearson

# Longman
# Vocabulary MENTOR JOY 3

**지은이** ｜ 교재개발연구소
**발행처** ｜ Pearson Education South Asia Pte Ltd.
**판매처** ｜ inkedu(inkbooks)

**전화** ｜ 02-455-9620(주문 및 고객지원)
**팩스** ｜ 02-455-9619
**등록** ｜ 제13-579호

**ISBN** ｜ 979-11-88228-21-8

잘못된 책은 구입처에서 바꿔 드립니다.

Longman

# Vocabulary
# MENTOR
# JOY

Social Words

**3**

Pearson

# Vocabulary

## 최신개정판 MENTOR JOY

Vocabulary MENTOR JOY 최신개정판 시리즈는 총 3권으로 구성되어 있으며, 각 권당 400단어로 총 1,200단어를 학습할 수 있습니다.

### | Book 1   Phonics Words

- 첫소리, 단모음, 장모음 등 소리에 따른 단어 구성
- 그림 제시를 통한 인지적 단어 학습
- 친절한 발음 설명을 통한 소리 학습
- 생생한 문장을 통한 자연스런 단어 학습

### | Book 2   Daily Words

- 일상생활과 연계된 주제별 단어로 구성
- 콜로케이션을 통한 실용적 단어 학습
- 단어, 콜로케이션에서 문장까지 확장 학습
- 문제풀이를 통한 자연스런 단어 학습

### | Book 3   Social Words

- 사회생활과 연계된 인문, 과학 등의 주제별 단어로 구성
- 콜로케이션을 통한 실용적 단어 학습
- 단어, 콜로케이션에서 문장까지 확장 학습
- 문제풀이를 통한 자연스런 단어 학습

# 영어발음기호표

영어를 시작하는 데 있어서 가장 기본은 영어 읽기입니다. 하지만 한글과 달리 영어는 소리와 철자가 완전히 일치하지 않기 때문에 단어를 올바르게 읽기가 쉽지 않습니다. 그래서 영단어의 소리를 제대로 표기한 발음기호표가 필요합니다. 『Vocabulary MENTOR JOY』에 첨부된 발음기호표를 통해 차근차근 영어의 발음기호를 읽는 법을 익히다 보면 영어 학습의 초석을 단단하게 다질 수 있을 것입니다.

## 모음

| 구분 | [a] | [e] | [i] | [o] | [u] | [ə] | [ʌ] | [ɔ] | [ɛ] | [æ] |
|------|-----|-----|-----|-----|-----|-----|-----|-----|-----|-----|
| 소리 | 아 | 에 | 이 | 오 | 우 | 어 | 어 | 오 | 에 | 애 |
| 기호 | ㅏ | ㅔ | ㅣ | ㅗ | ㅜ | ㅓ | ㅓ | ㅗ | ㅔ | ㅐ |

## 자음

### 1. 유성자음(16개)

| 구분 | [b] | [d] | [j] | [l] | [m] | [n] | [r] | [v] | [z] | [dʒ] | [ʒ] | [tz] | [ð] | [h] | [g] | [ŋ] |
|------|-----|-----|-----|-----|-----|-----|-----|-----|-----|------|-----|------|-----|-----|-----|-----|
| 소리 | 버 | 드 | 이 | 러 | 므 | 느 | 르 | 브 | 즈 | 쥐 | 지 | 쯔 | 뜨 | 흐 | 그 | 응 |
| 기호 | ㅂ | ㄷ | ㅣ | ㄹ | ㅁ | ㄴ | ㄹ | ㅂ | ㅈ | 주 | ㅈ | ㅉ | ㄸ | ㅎ | ㄱ | ㅇ |

### 2. 무성자음(10개)

| 구분 | [f] | [k] | [p] | [s] | [t] | [ʃ] | [tʃ] | [θ] | [t] | [ŋ] |
|------|-----|-----|-----|-----|-----|-----|------|-----|-----|-----|
| 소리 | 프 | 크 | 퍼 | 스 | 트 | 쉬 | 취 | 쓰 | 츠 | 응 |
| 기호 | ㅍ | ㅋ | ㅍ | ㅅ | ㅌ | 수 | 추 | ㅆ | ㅊ | ㅇ |

# How to Use This Book

실제 생활과 연계된 주제별 단어 400개를 학습할 수 있습니다. 특히, 콜로케이션을 통해 단어의 실제 쓰임을 자연스럽게 익힐 수 있습니다. 단어와 콜로케이션 소개, 써보기와 문제풀이 등으로 구성되어 있고, 스스로 복습할 수 있는 워크북도 함께 제공하고 있습니다.

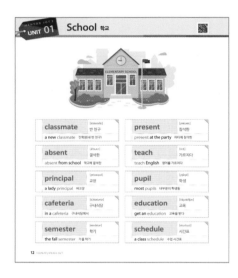

## Step 1

콜로케이션을 통해 단어의 일상적인 쓰임을 자연스럽게 익힐 수 있습니다. 또한 원어민의 발음을 통해서 단어의 정확한 소리를 확인할 수 있습니다.

## Step 2

콜로케이션과 함께 학습한 단어를 직접 써봄으로써 암기에도 효과적입니다.

# Step 3

문제 풀이를 통해 단어를 효과적으로 학습할 수 있습니다. 여기에 사용된 유용한 콜로케이션과 영어 문장들은 실제로 단어를 활용하는 데도 크게 도움이 될 수 있습니다.

# Step 4

유닛 5개가 끝나면 학습한 50개의 단어를 다시 한 번 확인할 수 있도록 리뷰 파트가 제공됩니다. 리뷰를 통해서 단어를 반복 학습할 수 있습니다.

# Step 5

제공된 워크북은 학생 스스로 단어를 학습할 수 있도록 구성하였습니다. 수업시간에 배운 단어를 집에서 복습할 수 있습니다.

# Syllabus

**Vocabulary Mentor JOY는 총 3권 1,200단어로 구성되어 있습니다**

1  학원 또는 학교 방과 후 수업 보조 교재로 사용 시에는 수업 종료 10분 전에 원어민의 발음을 들으면서 10개의 단어씩 학습합니다.

2  가정에서 스스로 학습 시에는 하루 10분 책과 함께 음원을 들으며 큰소리로 따라 읽으며 학습하고, 자기 전에 하루 10단어씩 복습합니다.

3  학원에서 보카 교재로 사용시(주 3회 수업), 저학년의 경우에는 하루 1개 유닛씩(권당 3개월 소요), 고학년의 경우에는 하루 2개 유닛씩(권당 2개월 소요) 학습합니다.

## 각 권의 학습 내용

| Unit | Book 1 | Book 2 | Book 3 |
|------|--------|--------|--------|
| 1 | b_ and p_ | Body  인체 | School  학교 |
| 2 | d_ and t_ | Family  가족 | Subjects  과목 |
| 3 | f_ and v_ | Friends  친구 | Tests  시험 |
| 4 | m_ and n_ | Personality  성격 | Homework  숙제 |
| 5 | h_ and j_ | Appearance  외모 | Supplies  소모품 |
| 6 | s_ and z_ | Emotions  감정 | Vacations  방학 |
| 7 | l_ and r_ | Senses  감각 | Field Trips  현장학습 |
| 8 | w_ and y_ | Health  건강 | Field Days  체육대회 |
| 9 | k_, _x and qu_ | Physiology  생리현상 | School Events  학교행사 |
| 10 | hard and soft c_ | House Things  집안 물건 | Campus Cleanup  교내미화 |
| 11 | hard and soft g_ | Kitchen Things  주방 물건 | Performances  공연 |
| 12 | short _a_ | Descriptions  사물 묘사 | Special Days  특별한 날 |
| 13 | short _e_ | Shapes  모양 | Jobs  직업 |
| 14 | short _i_ | Numbers & Quantities  수와 양 | Places  장소 |
| 15 | short _o_ | Positions  위치 | Cities & Nations  도시와 나라 |

# Contents

# School 학교

**01 classmate** [klǽsmèit] 반 친구

a new classmate　전학생(새 반 친구)

**02 present** [prézənt] 참석한

present **at the party**　파티에 참석한

**03 absent** [ǽbsənt] 결석한

absent **from school**　학교에 결석한

**04 teach** [tiːtʃ] 가르치다

teach **English**　영어를 가르치다

**05 principal** [prínsəpəl] 교장

a lady principal　여교장

**06 pupil** [pjúːpl] 학생

most pupils　대부분의 학생들

**07 cafeteria** [kæ̀fətíəriə] 구내식당

in a cafeteria　구내식당에서

**08 education** [èdʒukéiʃən] 교육

get an education　교육을 받다

**09 semester** [siméstər] 학기

the fall semester　가을 학기

**10 schedule** [skedʒuːl] 시간표

a class schedule　수업 시간표

✎ 영어 단어를 완성하세요.

**1** classmate 반 친구

→ c ☐ assmate    cla ☐ s ☐ ate    ☐ | ☐

**2** present 참석한

→ p ☐ esent    pr ☐ se ☐ t    ☐ | ☐

**3** absent 결석한

→ ab ☐ ent    a ☐ sen ☐    ☐ | ☐

**4** teach 가르치다

→ t ☐ ach    tea ☐ ☐    ☐ | ☐

**5** principal 교장

→ princip ☐ l    pri ☐ ci ☐ al    ☐ | ☐

**6** pupil 학생

→ ☐ upil    p ☐ p ☐ l    ☐ | ☐

**7** cafeteria 구내식당

→ cafeter ☐ a    ca ☐ teria    ☐ | ☐

**8** education 교육

→ edu ☐ ation    e ☐ cation    ☐ | ☐

**9** semester 학기

→ semes ☐ er    se ☐ ster    ☐ | ☐

**10** schedule 시간표

→ sche ☐ ule    s ☐ edule    ☐ | ☐

# Practice

**A** 단어의 알맞은 뜻을 선으로 연결한 후, 빈칸에 단어를 직접 써보세요.

| | | | |
|---|---|---|---|
| 1 | pupil | • • 교장 | → |
| 2 | classmate | • • 학생 | → |
| 3 | teach | • • 반 친구 | → |
| 4 | principal | • • 구내식당 | → |
| 5 | cafeteria | • • 가르치다 | → |

**B** 우리말과 일치하도록 빈칸에 알맞은 단어를 보기 에서 찾아 쓰세요.

보기  present    education    schedule    absent    semester

1  학교에 결석한  →  _____ from school

2  파티에 참석한  →  _____ at the party

3  교육을 받다  →  get an _____

4  가을 학기  →  the fall _____

5  수업 시간표  →  a class _____

**C** 우리말을 참고해서 빈칸에 알맞은 단어를 골라 문장을 완성하세요.

1 He is often _____ from school. 그는 종종 학교에 **결석한다.**
( absent / present )

2 She _____ English to them. 그녀는 그들에게 영어를 **가르친다.**
( teaches / pupils )

3 Did you check your class _____ ? 너는 수업 **시간표**를 확인했니?
( schedule / semester )

4 We have a new _____ today. 오늘 전학생(새 **반 친구**)이 왔다.
( cafeteria / classmate )

5 The lady _____ is very strict. 그 여**교장**은 매우 엄격하다.
( classmate / principal )

**D** 우리말을 참고해서 알맞은 단어를 넣어 문장을 완성하세요.

1 Most p_____s learn a musical instrument.
대부분의 **학생들**은 악기를 배운다.

2 They are eating in a c_____.
그들은 **구내식당**에서 식사하고 있다.

3 I was p_____ at the party yesterday.
나는 어제 그 파티에 **참석했**다.

4 The fall s_____ begins in September.
가을 **학기**는 9월에 시작한다.

5 Your children will get a good e_____.
너의 아이들은 좋은 **교육**을 받을 것이다.

# Subjects 과목

| 01 **subject** | [sʌ́bdʒikt / sʌbdʒékt] 과목 |
|---|---|
| my favorite subject | 내가 가장 좋아하는 과목 |

| 02 **science** | [sáiəns] 과학 |
|---|---|
| a science teacher | 과학 선생님 |

| 03 **music** | [mjúːzik] 음악 |
|---|---|
| music class | 음악 수업 |

| 04 **history** | [hístəri] 역사 |
|---|---|
| a history book | 역사책 |

| 05 **art** | [ɑːrt] 미술 |
|---|---|
| modern art | 현대 미술 |

| 06 **learn** | [ləːrn] 배우다 |
|---|---|
| learn to use | 사용법을 배우다 |

| 07 **understand** | [ʌ̀ndərstǽnd] 이해하다 |
|---|---|
| hard to understand | 이해하기 어려운 |

| 08 **lesson** | [lésən] 레슨, 수업 |
|---|---|
| take lessons | 레슨을 받다 |

| 09 **curriculum** | [kəríkjələm] 교육과정 |
|---|---|
| the school curriculum | 학교 교육과정 |

| 10 **tutor** | [tjúːtər] 가정교사 |
|---|---|
| a math tutor | 수학 가정교사 |

✎ 영어 단어를 완성하세요.

**1**  subject 과목

→  sub[ ]ect    [ ]bject    [ ][ ]

**2**  science 과학

→  [ ]cience    s[ ]ence    [ ][ ]

**3**  music 음악

→  musi[ ]    [ ]sic    [ ][ ]

**4**  history 역사

→  h[ ]story    hi[ ]ory    [ ][ ]

**5**  art 미술

→  [ ]rt    a[ ]    [ ][ ]

**6**  learn 배우다

→  lea[ ]n    [ ]ear[ ]    [ ][ ]

**7**  understand 이해하다

→  [ ]nderstand    un[ ]ers[ ]and    [ ][ ]

**8**  lesson 레슨, 수업

→  le[ ]son    [ ]ess[ ]n    [ ][ ]

**9**  curriculum 교육과정

→  curric[ ]lum    [ ]urriculu[ ]    [ ][ ]

**10**  tutor 가정교사

→  tut[ ]r    [ ]tor    [ ][ ]

# Practice

A   단어의 알맞은 뜻을 선으로 연결한 후, 빈칸에 단어를 직접 써보세요.

| 1 | art | • | • | 과학 | → | |
| 2 | music | • | • | 미술 | → | |
| 3 | lesson | • | • | 음악 | → | |
| 4 | science | • | • | 역사 | → | |
| 5 | history | • | • | 레슨, 수업 | → | |

B   우리말과 일치하도록 빈칸에 알맞은 단어를 보기 에서 찾아 쓰세요.

보기   learn   tutor   subject   understand   curriculum

1   사용법을 배우다   →   _____ to use

2   수학 가정교사   →   a math _____

3   이해하기 어려운   →   hard to _____

4   학교 교육과정   →   the school _____

5   내가 가장 좋아하는 과목   →   my favorite _____

**C** 우리말을 참고해서 빈칸에 알맞은 단어를 골라 문장을 완성하세요.

1 Mr. Johnson is a _____ teacher. Johnson 씨는 **과학** 선생님이다.
( history / science )

2 My favorite _____ is English. 내가 가장 좋아하는 **과목**은 영어다.
( tutor / subject )

3 I'm taking guitar _____. 나는 기타 **레슨**을 받고 있다.
( lessons / curriculum )

4 I am not interested in modern _____. 나는 현대 **미술**에는 관심이 없다.
( art / music )

5 The questions were hard to _____. 그 질문들은 **이해하기** 어려웠다.
( learn / understand )

**D** 우리말을 참고해서 알맞은 단어를 넣어 문장을 완성하세요.

1 What did you do in m_____ class today?
너는 오늘 **음악** 수업에서 뭘 했니?

2 She read a lot of h_____ books.
그녀는 **역사책**을 많이 읽었다.

3 He must study with his math t_____.
그는 수학 **가정교사**와 공부해야 한다.

4 English is a part of the school c_____.
영어는 학교 **교육과정**의 일부다.

5 They l_____ to use computer programs.
그들은 컴퓨터 프로그램 사용법을 **배운다**.

# Tests 시험

| 01 **pass** | [pæs] 합격하다 |
|---|---|
| pass the test  시험에 합격하다 | |

| 02 **fail** | [feil] 낙제하다 |
|---|---|
| fail the interview  면접에 낙제하다 | |

| 03 **answer** | [ǽnsər] 답, 해답 |
|---|---|
| an answer sheet  답안지 | |

| 04 **examination** | [igzæmənéiʃən] 시험 |
|---|---|
| take an examination  시험을 치르다 | |

| 05 **score** | [skɔːr] 점수 |
|---|---|
| make a score  점수를 받다 | |

| 06 **grade** | [greid] 성적, 학년 |
|---|---|
| my math grades  나의 수학 성적 | |

| 07 **easy** | [íːzi] 쉬운 |
|---|---|
| an easy problem  쉬운 문제 | |

| 08 **difficult** | [dífikʌ̀lt] 어려운 |
|---|---|
| a difficult task  어려운 과제 | |

| 09 **cheat** | [tʃiːt] 부정행위 하다 |
|---|---|
| cheat on an exam  시험에서 부정행위 하다 | |

| 10 **finish** | [fíniʃ] 끝내다 |
|---|---|
| finish the report  보고서를 끝내다 | |

✎ 영어 단어를 완성하세요.

1  pass 합격하다
   → pa ☐ s      ☐ ☐ ss      ☐ ☐

2  fail 낙제하다
   → ☐ ail       f ☐ l       ☐ ☐

3  answer 답, 해답
   → ans ☐ er    answ ☐      ☐ ☐

4  examination 시험
   → exam ☐ nation    ☐ amination    ☐ ☐

5  score 점수
   → s ☐ ore     sc ☐ e      ☐ ☐

6  grade 성적, 학년
   → gra ☐ e     g ☐ ad      ☐ ☐

7  easy 쉬운
   → ☐ asy       ea ☐        ☐ ☐

8  difficult 어려운
   → diffic ☐ lt    dif ☐ cult    ☐ ☐

9  cheat 부정행위 하다
   → ch ☐ at     ☐ eat       ☐ ☐

10  finish 끝내다
   → ☐ inish     fini ☐      ☐ ☐

# Practice

**A**  단어의 알맞은 뜻을 선으로 연결한 후, 빈칸에 단어를 직접 써보세요.

| | | | |
|---|---|---|---|
| 1 | fail • | • 점수 | → _____ |
| 2 | pass • | • 쉬운 | → _____ |
| 3 | easy • | • 답, 해답 | → _____ |
| 4 | score • | • 합격하다 | → _____ |
| 5 | answer • | • 낙제하다 | → _____ |

**B**  우리말과 일치하도록 빈칸에 알맞은 단어를 보기 에서 찾아 쓰세요.

보기    cheat    finish    grade    difficult    examination

1  보고서를 끝내다  →  _____ the report

2  나의 수학 성적  →  my math _____ s

3  시험에서 부정행위 하다  →  _____ on an exam

4  어려운 과제  →  a _____ task

5  시험을 치르다  →  take an _____

**C** 우리말을 참고해서 빈칸에 알맞은 단어를 골라 문장을 완성하세요.

1 My math _____ are poor. 나의 수학 **성적**은 안 좋다.
( grades / examinations )

2 I didn't _____ the interview. 나는 면접에 **낙제하지** 않았다.
( pass / fail )

3 He _____ on the exam. 그는 시험에서 **부정행위를 했다**.
( cheated / finished )

4 Hand in your _____ sheets, please. 여러분의 **답**안지를 제출하세요.
( score / answer )

5 This is not an _____ problem. 이것은 **쉬운** 문제가 아니다.
( easy / difficult )


**D** 우리말을 참고해서 알맞은 단어를 넣어 문장을 완성하세요.

1 I made a s_____ of 90.
나는 90**점**을 받았다.

2 I hope you will p_____ the test.
나는 네가 시험에 **합격하길** 바란다.

3 It was a d_____ task.
그것은 **어려운** 과제였다.

4 You must f_____ the report by tomorrow.
너는 그 보고서를 내일까지 **끝내야** 한다.

5 Did you take the e_____ yesterday?
너는 어제 **시험을** 봤니?

# Homework 숙제

| 01 | **homework** | [hóumwə̀ːrk] 숙제 |
|---|---|---|
| | do my homework  숙제를 하다 | |

| 02 | **review** | [rivjúː] 복습하다 |
|---|---|---|
| | review the textbook  교과서를 복습하다 | |

| 03 | **example** | [igzǽmpl] 예, 본보기 |
|---|---|---|
| | give an example  예를 들다 | |

| 04 | **study** | [stʌ́di] 공부하다 |
|---|---|---|
| | study for an exam  시험 공부하다 | |

| 05 | **advice** | [ədváis / ædváis] 충고 |
|---|---|---|
| | a piece of advice  충고 하나 | |

| 06 | **effort** | [éfərt] 노력 |
|---|---|---|
| | make an effort  노력하다 | |

| 07 | **group** | [gruːp] 그룹, 모임 |
|---|---|---|
| | work in groups  그룹으로 작업하다 | |

| 08 | **problem** | [prábləm] 문제 |
|---|---|---|
| | solve a problem  문제를 풀다 | |

| 09 | **excuse** | [ikskjúːs] 변명 |
|---|---|---|
| | make an excuse  변명하다 | |

| 10 | **explain** | [ikspléin] 설명하다 |
|---|---|---|
| | difficult to explain  설명하기 어려운 | |

영어 단어를 완성하세요.

**1** homework 숙제

→ home ork  ho ewo k

**2** review 복습하다

→ rev ew  e iew

**3** example 예, 본보기

→ exa ple  ample

**4** study 공부하다

→ stu y  s dy

**5** advice 충고

→ ad ice  vice

**6** effort 노력

→ e fort  eff t

**7** group 그룹, 모임

→ gro p  oup

**8** problem 문제

→ p oblem  pro em

**9** excuse 변명

→ ex use  cuse

**10** explain 설명하다

→ explai  ex ain

# Practice

A 단어의 알맞은 뜻을 선으로 연결한 후, 빈칸에 단어를 직접 써보세요.

1 study • • 변명 →

2 review • • 충고 →

3 group • • 공부하다 →

4 advice • • 복습하다 →

5 excuse • • 그룹, 모임 →

B 우리말과 일치하도록 빈칸에 알맞은 단어를 보기 에서 찾아 쓰세요.

보기　effort　explain　problem　example　homework

1 노력하다 → make an _____

2 예를 들다 → give an _____

3 숙제를 하다 → do my _____

4 문제를 풀다 → solve a _____

5 설명하기 어려운 → difficult to _____

**C** 우리말을 참고해서 빈칸에 알맞은 단어를 골라 문장을 완성하세요.

1 I did my _____. 나는 **숙제**를 했다.
   ( homework / problem )

2 We will work in _____. 우리는 **그룹**으로 작업할 거다.
   ( efforts / groups )

3 Did you _____ for the exam? 너는 시험 **공부했니**?
   ( study / review )

4 Let me give you an _____. 내가 **예**를 하나 들어보죠.
   ( explain / example )

5 He gave me a piece of _____. 그는 나에게 **충고** 하나 했다.
   ( advice / excuse )

**D** 우리말을 참고해서 알맞은 단어를 넣어 문장을 완성하세요.

1 We should r_____ the textbook.
   우리는 교과서를 **복습하는** 게 좋겠다.

2 It is difficult to e_____.
   그것은 **설명하기** 어렵다.

3 We tried to solve the p_____.
   우리는 그 **문제**를 풀려고 시도했다.

4 I made an e_____ to get an A.
   나는 A를 받으려고 **노력**했다.

5 She made an e_____ for herself.
   그녀는 자신을 위해 **변명**했다.

# Supplies 소모품

| 01 **stationery** | [stéiʃənèri] 문구류 |
|---|---|
| a stationery store 문구점 | |

| 02 **stapler** | [stéiplər] 스테이플러 |
|---|---|
| my own stapler 내 스테이플러 | |

| 03 **chalk** | [tʃɔːk] 분필 |
|---|---|
| a piece of chalk 분필 한 개 | |

| 04 **sketchbook** | [skétʃbùk] 스케치북 |
|---|---|
| in my sketchbook 내 스케치북에 | |

| 05 **album** | [ǽlbəm] 앨범 |
|---|---|
| a stamp album 우표 앨범 | |

| 06 **clipboard** | [klípbɔ̀ːrd] 클립보드 |
|---|---|
| a new clipboard 새 클립보드 | |

| 07 **compass** | [kʌ́mpəs] 나침반 |
|---|---|
| a map and compass 지도와 나침반 | |

| 08 **folder** | [fóuldər] 폴더 |
|---|---|
| in a folder 폴더에 | |

| 09 **highlighter** | [háilàitər] 형광펜 |
|---|---|
| with a highlighter 형광펜으로 | |

| 10 **scissors** | [sízərz] 가위 |
|---|---|
| a pair of scissors 가위 한 자루 | |

✎ 영어 단어를 완성하세요.

**1** stationery 문구류

→ statione [ ] y    sta [ ] onery    [ ] [ ]

**2** stapler 스테이플러

→ s [ ] apler    sta [ ] er    [ ] [ ]

**3** chalk 분필

→ cha [ ] k    [ ] alk    [ ] [ ]

**4** sketchbook 스케치북

→ ske [ ] chbook    [ ] etchbook    [ ] [ ]

**5** album 앨범

→ al [ ] um    alb [ ]    [ ] [ ]

**6** clipboard 클립보드

→ cli [ ] board    clipb [ ] rd    [ ] [ ]

**7** compass 나침반

→ com [ ] ass    c [ ] pass    [ ] [ ]

**8** folder 폴더

→ f [ ] lder    [ ] ol [ ] er    [ ] [ ]

**9** highlighter 형광펜

→ [ ] ighlighter    hi [ ] lighter    [ ] [ ]

**10** scissors 가위

→ scissor [ ]    [ ] issors    [ ] [ ]

# Practice

**A** 단어의 알맞은 뜻을 선으로 연결한 후, 빈칸에 단어를 직접 써보세요.

| | | | | |
|---|---|---|---|---|
| 1 | chalk • | • 앨범 | → | |
| 2 | album • | • 폴더 | → | |
| 3 | stapler • | • 분필 | → | |
| 4 | folder • | • 나침반 | → | |
| 5 | compass • | • 스테이플러 | → | |

**B** 우리말과 일치하도록 빈칸에 알맞은 단어를 보기 에서 찾아 쓰세요.

보기    scissors    clipboard    stationery    sketchbook    highlighter

1  새 클립보드 → a new _____

2  가위 한 자루 → a pair of _____

3  내 스케치북에 → in my _____

4  문구점 → a _____ store

5  형광펜으로 → with a _____

**C** 우리말을 참고해서 빈칸에 알맞은 단어를 골라 문장을 완성하세요.

1 Bring me a piece of _____. 내게 **분필** 한 개 갖다 줘.
  ( chalk / highlighter )

2 We need to buy a new _____. 우리는 새 **클립보드**를 사야겠다.
  ( folder / clipboard )

3 I draw pictures in my _____. 나는 **스케치북**에 그림을 그린다.
  ( album / sketchbook )

4 He handed me a pair of _____. 그는 나에게 **가위** 한 자루를 건넸다.
  ( scissors / stapler )

5 Is there a _____ store around here? 이 근처에 **문구**점이 있니?
  ( compass / stationery )

**D** 우리말을 참고해서 알맞은 단어를 넣어 문장을 완성하세요.

1 I bought a stamp a_____. 나는 우표 **앨범**을 샀다.

2 Please keep these in the f_____. 이것들을 그 **폴더**에 보관하세요.

3 I don't have my own s_____. 나는 **스테이플러**도 없다.

4 Take a map and c_____ with you. 지도와 **나침반**을 갖고 가라.

5 Underline the word with a h_____. 그 단어에 **형광펜**으로 밑줄을 쳐라.

## A 다음 영어 단어의 우리말 뜻을 쓰세요.

1 art → _____    2 chalk → _____

3 pupil → _____    4 stapler → _____

5 absent → _____    6 principal → _____

7 homework → _____    8 classmate → _____

9 history → _____    10 highlighter → _____

11 semester → _____    12 scissors → _____

13 difficult → _____    14 education → _____

## B 다음 우리말을 보고 영어표현을 완성하세요.

1 a stamp a _____
우표 앨범

2 an e _____ problem
쉬운 문제

3 t _____ English
영어를 가르치다

4 l _____ to use
사용법을 배우다

5 s _____ for an exam
시험 공부하다

6 a map and c _____
지도와 나침반

7 p _____ the test
시험에 합격하다

8 make an e _____
노력하다

9 my math g _____ s
나의 수학 성적

10 an a _____ sheet
답안지

11 c _____ on an exam
시험에서 부정행위 하다

12 f _____ the report
보고서를 끝내다

13 a math t _____
수학 가정교사

14 difficult to e _____
설명하기 어려운

**C** 우리말과 같도록 괄호 안에서 알맞은 단어에 동그라미 하세요.

1 Mr. Johnson is a ( science / history ) teacher. Johnson 씨는 **과학** 선생님이다.

2 Let me give you an ( answer / example ). 내가 **예**를 하나 들어보죠.

3 I didn't ( pass / fail ) the interview. 나는 면접에 **낙제하지** 않았다.

4 I made a ( grade / score ) of 90. 나는 90**점**을 받았다.

5 I'm taking guitar ( lessons / subjects ). 나는 기타 **레슨**을 받고 있다.

6 I was ( absent / present ) at the party yesterday. 나는 어제 그 파티에 **참석했**다.

7 Did you take the ( examination / curriculum ) yesterday? 너는 어제 **시험을** 봤니?

8 She made an ( excuse / group ) for herself. 그녀는 자신을 위해 **변명**했다.

**D** 우리말과 같도록 다음 영어 문장을 완성하세요.

1 He gave me a piece of a_____. 그는 나에게 **충고** 하나 했다.

2 My favorite s_____ is English. 내가 가장 좋아하는 **과목**은 영어다.

3 What did you do in m_____ class today? 너는 오늘 **음악** 수업에서 뭘 했니?

4 Please keep these in the f_____. 이것들을 그 **폴더**에 보관하세요.

5 We should r_____ the textbook. 우리는 교과서를 **복습하는** 게 좋겠다.

6 They are eating in a c_____. 그들은 **구내식당**에서 식사하고 있다.

7 The questions were hard to u_____. 그 질문들은 **이해하기** 어려웠다.

8 We tried to solve the p_____. 우리는 그 **문제**를 풀려고 시도했다.

# Vacations 방학

| 01 **vacation** [veikéiʃən] 방학 |
| --- |
| the summer vacation  여름방학 |

| 02 **wonderful** [wʌ́ndərfəl] 아주 멋진 |
| --- |
| a wonderful time  아주 멋진 시간 |

| 03 **country** [kʌ́ntri] 시골 |
| --- |
| live in the country  시골에서 살다 |

| 04 **wait** [weit] 기다리다 |
| --- |
| wait for spring  봄을 기다리다 |

| 05 **during** [djúəriŋ] ~ 동안 |
| --- |
| during the winter  겨울 동안 |

| 06 **forget** [fərgét] 잊다 |
| --- |
| forget to write back  답장하는 것을 잊다 |

| 07 **remember** [rimémbər] 기억하다 |
| --- |
| remember it clearly  그것을 확실히 기억하다 |

| 08 **planner** [plǽnər] 계획표 |
| --- |
| a vacation planner  방학 계획표 |

| 09 **participate** [pɑːrtísəpèit] 참여하다 |
| --- |
| participate in an activity  활동에 참여하다 |

| 10 **leisure** [líːʒər] 여가 |
| --- |
| my leisure activity  내 여가 활동 |

✎ 영어 단어를 완성하세요.

**1** vacation 방학

→ ⬜ acation　　va ⬜ tion　　⬜⬜⬜⬜⬜⬜⬜⬜

**2** wonderful 아주 멋진

→ wonder ⬜ ul　　⬜ nderful　　⬜⬜⬜⬜⬜⬜⬜⬜

**3** country 시골

→ cou ⬜ try　　c ⬜ ntry　　⬜⬜⬜⬜⬜⬜⬜⬜

**4** wait 기다리다

→ wa ⬜ t　　⬜ it　　⬜⬜⬜⬜⬜⬜⬜⬜

**5** during ~동안

→ durin ⬜　　d ⬜ ing　　⬜⬜⬜⬜⬜⬜⬜⬜

**6** forget 잊다

→ ⬜ orget　　for ⬜ t　　⬜⬜⬜⬜⬜⬜⬜⬜

**7** remember 기억하다

→ remem ⬜ er　　re ⬜ mber　　⬜⬜⬜⬜⬜⬜⬜⬜

**8** planner 계획표

→ plan ⬜ er　　⬜ anner　　⬜⬜⬜⬜⬜⬜⬜⬜

**9** participate 참여하다

→ pa ⬜ ticipate　　parti ⬜ pate　　⬜⬜⬜⬜⬜⬜⬜⬜

**10** leisure 여가

→ lei ⬜ ure　　l ⬜ sure　　⬜⬜⬜⬜⬜⬜⬜⬜

# ✎ Practice

**A** 단어의 알맞은 뜻을 선으로 연결한 후, 빈칸에 단어를 직접 써보세요.

1 wait • • 여가 →

2 forget • • 방학 →

3 leisure • • 잊다 →

4 vacation • • 기억하다 →

5 remember • • 기다리다 →

**B** 우리말과 일치하도록 빈칸에 알맞은 단어를 보기 에서 찾아 쓰세요.

보기   during   planner   country   wonderful   participate

1 방학 계획표 → a vacation _____

2 겨울 동안 → _____ the winter

3 아주 멋진 시간 → a _____ time

4 시골에서 살다 → live in the _____

5 활동에 참여하다 → _____ in an activity

**C** 우리말을 참고해서 빈칸에 알맞은 단어를 골라 문장을 완성하세요.

1   Don't _____ to write back to me. 나에게 답장하는 것을 **잊지** 마라.
( forget / remember )

2   We had a _____ time. 우리는 **아주 멋진** 시간을 보냈다.
( leisure / wonderful )

3   I _____ for spring to come. 나는 봄이 오기를 **기다린다**.
( wait / planner )

4   Did you enjoy your summer _____? 너는 여름**방학**이 즐거웠니?
( country / vacation )

5   I want to _____ in this activity. 나는 이 활동에 **참여하고** 싶다.
( during / participate )

**D** 우리말을 참고해서 알맞은 단어를 넣어 문장을 완성하세요.

1   I want to live in the c_____. 나는 **시골**에서 살고 싶다.

2   I r_____ it clearly. 나는 그것을 확실히 **기억한다**.

3   I will make a vacation p_____. 나는 방학 **계획표**를 만들 거다.

4   Watching TV is my l_____ activity. TV 시청이 내 **여가** 활동이다.

5   She is at home d_____ the winter. 그녀는 겨울 **동안** 집에 있다.

# Field Trips 현장학습

| 01 | **picnic** | [píknik]<br>소풍 |
|---|---|---|
| | go on a picnic 소풍을 가다 | |

| 02 | **basket** | [bǽskit]<br>바구니 |
|---|---|---|
| | a picnic basket 소풍 바구니 | |

| 03 | **contest** | [kántest]<br>대회 |
|---|---|---|
| | a talent contest 장기자랑 대회 | |

| 04 | **happen** | [hǽpən]<br>일어나다 |
|---|---|---|
| | happen to me 나에게 일어나다 | |

| 05 | **hurry** | [hə́:ri]<br>서두르다 |
|---|---|---|
| | hurry up and go 서둘러 가다 | |

| 06 | **leave** | [li:v]<br>떠나다 |
|---|---|---|
| | leave soon 곧 떠나다 | |

| 07 | **pick** | [pik]<br>(꽃을) 꺾다 |
|---|---|---|
| | pick flowers 꽃을 꺾다 | |

| 08 | **special** | [spéʃəl]<br>특별한 |
|---|---|---|
| | a special friend 특별한 친구 | |

| 09 | **activity** | [æktívəti]<br>활동 |
|---|---|---|
| | an outdoor activity 야외활동 | |

| 10 | **volunteer** | [vàləntíər]<br>지원자 |
|---|---|---|
| | need a volunteer 지원자가 필요하다 | |

✎ 영어 단어를 완성하세요.

**1** picnic 소풍

→ [ ]icnic  pi[ ]ic  [ ][ ]

**2** basket 바구니

→ b[ ]sket  ba[ ]et  [ ][ ]

**3** contest 대회

→ conte[ ]t  [ ]ntest  [ ]

**4** happen 일어나다

→ [ ]appen  h[ ]pen  [ ]

**5** hurry 서두르다

→ hurr[ ]  h[ ]ry  [ ]

**6** leave 떠나다

→ lea[ ]e  l[ ]ve  [ ]

**7** pick (꽃을) 꺾다

→ pic[ ]  p[ ]k  [ ]

**8** special 특별한

→ spe[ ]ial  [ ]ecial  [ ]

**9** activity 활동

→ activ[ ]ty  a[ ]ivity  [ ]

**10** volunteer 지원자

→ voluntee[ ]  vol[ ]teer  [ ]

# Practice

**A** 단어의 알맞은 뜻을 선으로 연결한 후, 빈칸에 단어를 직접 써보세요.

| 1 | pick | • | | • | 소풍 | → | |
| 2 | picnic | • | | • | 대회 | → | |
| 3 | contest | • | | • | 활동 | → | |
| 4 | basket | • | | • | 바구니 | → | |
| 5 | activity | • | | • | (꽃을) 꺾다 | → | |

**B** 우리말과 일치하도록 빈칸에 알맞은 단어를 보기 에서 찾아 쓰세요.

보기    leave    hurry    happen    special    volunteer

1 서둘러 가다 → ＿＿＿＿＿ up and go

2 곧 떠나다 → ＿＿＿＿＿ soon

3 특별한 친구 → a ＿＿＿＿＿ friend

4 나에게 일어나다 → ＿＿＿＿＿ to me

5 지원자가 필요하다 → need a ＿＿＿＿＿

**C** 우리말을 참고해서 빈칸에 알맞은 단어를 골라 문장을 완성하세요.

1 Let's go on a _____ today. 오늘 **소풍** 가자.
   ( picnic / contest )

2 Let's _____ up and go home. **서둘러** 집에 가자.
   ( leave / hurry )

3 An odd thing _____ to me. 희한한 일이 나에게 **일어났다**.
   ( picked / happened )

4 Kate is a very _____ friend. Kate는 매우 **특별한** 친구다.
   ( basket / special )

5 Camping is a fun outdoor _____. 캠핑은 재미있는 야외**활동**이다.
   ( activity / volunteer )


**D** 우리말을 참고해서 알맞은 단어를 넣어 문장을 완성하세요.

1 Where did you  p _____ the flowers?
   너는 그 꽃들을 어디에서 **꺾었니**?

2 He is dancing in the talent  c _____.
   그는 장기자랑 **대회**에서 춤추고 있다.

3 We will have to  l _____ soon.
   우리는 곧 **떠나야** 할 거다.

4 We need a  v _____ for this game.
   우리는 이 게임에 **지원자**가 필요하다.

5 She brought her lunch in a picnic  b _____.
   그녀는 점심을 소풍 **바구니**에 가져왔다.

# UNIT 08    Field Days 체육대회

**01 march** [mɑːrtʃ]
행진하다
march to City Hall   시청까지 행진하다

**02 field** [fiːld]
경기장
a sports field   운동 경기장

**03 playground** [pléigràund]
운동장
a school playground   학교 운동장

**04 match** [mætʃ]
경기, 시합
a big match   큰 경기

**05 winner** [wínər]
승자
the winner of a game   게임의 승자

**06 cheer** [tʃiər]
응원하다
cheer for our players   우리 선수들을 응원하다

**07 medal** [médəl]
메달
win a gold medal   금메달을 따다

**08 block** [blɑk]
막다
block a shot   슛을 막다

**09 loser** [lúːzər]
패자
a good loser   깨끗이 승복하는 패자

**10 whistle** [hwísl]
호루라기
blow a whistle   호루라기를 불다

✎ 영어 단어를 완성하세요.

1 **march** 행진하다

→ m ⬜ rch    mar ⬜    ⬜ ⬜

2 **field** 경기장

→ fie ⬜ d    f ⬜ ld    ⬜ ⬜

3 **playground** 운동장

→ p ⬜ ayground    play ⬜ ound    ⬜

4 **match** 경기, 시합

→ matc ⬜    m ⬜ ch    ⬜

5 **winner** 승자

→ wi ⬜ ner    ⬜ nner    ⬜

6 **cheer** 응원하다

→ che ⬜ r    ⬜ eer    ⬜ ⬜

7 **medal** 메달

→ m ⬜ dal    me ⬜ l    ⬜ ⬜

8 **block** 막다

→ bl ⬜ ck    ⬜ ock    ⬜ ⬜

9 **loser** 패자

→ ⬜ oser    lo ⬜ r    ⬜ ⬜

10 **whistle** 호루라기

→ whis ⬜ le    ⬜ istle    ⬜ ⬜

# Practice

**A** 단어의 알맞은 뜻을 선으로 연결한 후, 빈칸에 단어를 직접 써보세요.

| 1 | match | • | | • | 승자 | → | |
| 2 | block | • | | • | 경기, 시합 | → | |
| 3 | loser | • | | • | 막다 | → | |
| 4 | cheer | • | | • | 패자 | → | |
| 5 | winner | • | | • | 응원하다 | → | |

**B** 우리말과 일치하도록 빈칸에 알맞은 단어를 보기 에서 찾아 쓰세요.

> 보기    medal    field    march    whistle    playground

1   운동 경기장   →   a sports _____

2   호루라기를 불다   →   blow a _____

3   학교 운동장   →   a school _____

4   금메달을 따다   →   win a gold _____

5   시청까지 행진하다   →   _____ to City Hall

**C** 우리말을 참고해서 빈칸에 알맞은 단어를 골라 문장을 완성하세요.

1 James is the _____ of this game. James는 이 게임의 **승자**다.
( loser / winner )

2 This city has a large sports _____. 이 도시에는 큰 운동 **경기장**이 있다.
( field / playground )

3 The goalkeeper _____ the shot. 그 골키퍼는 슛을 **막았다**.
( cheered / blocked )

4 We will _____ to City Hall. 우리는 시청까지 **행진할** 거다.
( march / match )

5 I'm happy to win a gold _____. 나는 금**메달**을 따서 기쁘다.
( medal / whistle )

**D** 우리말을 참고해서 알맞은 단어를 넣어 문장을 완성하세요.

1 Let's c _____ for our players! 우리 선수들을 **응원하자**!

2 He is not a good l _____. 그는 깨끗이 승복하는 **패자**가 아니다.

3 They gathered on the school p _____. 그들은 그 학교 **운동장**에 모였다.

4 There will be a big m _____ tomorrow. 내일 큰 **경기**가 있을 거다.

5 The referee blew the w _____. 그 심판은 **호루라기**를 불었다.

# School Events 학교행사

**01 enter** [éntər] 입학하다

enter a school 학교에 입학하다

**02 congratulation** [kəngrætʃuléiʃən] 축하

a letter of congratulation 축하 편지

**03 memory** [méməri] 기억

a clear memory 선명한 기억

**04 graduate** [grǽdʒuèit] 졸업하다

graduate from Harvard 하버드를 졸업하다

**05 proud** [praud] 자랑스러운

proud of myself 내 자신이 자랑스러운

**06 beginning** [bigíniŋ] 초반, 시작

in the beginning 처음에는

**07 honor** [ánər] 우등, 명예

win an honor prize 우등상을 타다

**08 kindergarten** [kíndərgàːrtən] 유치원

go to kindergarten 유치원에 다니다

**09 elementary** [èləméntəri] 초등의

elementary students 초등학생들

**10 university** [jùːnəvə́ːrsəti] 대학

a university professor 대학 교수

✎ 영어 단어를 완성하세요.

1   enter 입학하다
    →    ☐nter        e☐er        ☐ ☐

2   congratulation 축하
    →    con☐ratulation    ☐ngratulation    ☐ ☐

3   memory 기억
    →    memor☐        me☐ry        ☐ ☐

4   graduate 졸업하다
    →    grad☐ate        ☐aduate        ☐ ☐

5   proud 자랑스러운
    →    prou☐        ☐oud        ☐ ☐

6   beginning 초반, 시작
    →    beginni☐g        be☐nning        ☐ ☐

7   honor 우등, 명예
    →    ho☐or        ☐nor        ☐ ☐

8   kindergarten 유치원
    →    kindergar☐en        kinde☐arten        ☐ ☐

9   elementary 초등의
    →    ele☐entary        ☐ementary        ☐ ☐

10  university 대학
    →    univers☐ty        ☐iversity        ☐ ☐

# Practice

**A** 단어의 알맞은 뜻을 선으로 연결한 후, 빈칸에 단어를 직접 써보세요.

1 enter •          • 졸업하다 →

2 proud •          • 입학하다 →

3 honor •          • 기억 →

4 memory •          • 우등, 명예 →

5 graduate •        • 자랑스러운 →

**B** 우리말과 일치하도록 빈칸에 알맞은 단어를 보기 에서 찾아 쓰세요.

보기   university  beginning  kindergarten  elementary  congratulation

1 처음에는          → in the _____

2 대학 교수          → a _____ professor

3 초등학생들          → _____ students

4 유치원에 다니다       → go to _____

5 축하 편지          → a letter of _____

**C** 우리말을 참고해서 빈칸에 알맞은 단어를 골라 문장을 완성하세요.

1 Tom _____ a music school. Tom은 음악학교에 **입학했다**.
( entered / graduated )

2 They are _____ students. 그들은 **초등**학생들이다.
( university / elementary )

3 I was glad to win an _____ prize. 나는 **우등**상을 타서 기뻤다.
( honor / memory )

4 My sister goes to _____. 내 여동생은 **유치원**에 다닌다.
( beginning / kindergarten )

5 I sent him a letter of _____. 나는 그에게 **축하** 편지를 보냈다.
( proud / congratulation )


**D** 우리말을 참고해서 알맞은 단어를 넣어 문장을 완성하세요.

1 I am p_____ of myself.
나는 내 자신이 **자랑스럽**다.

2 My father is a u_____ professor.
나의 아버지는 **대학** 교수다.

3 In the b_____, I didn't like you.
**처음**에는 내가 너를 좋아하지 않았다.

4 He will g_____ from Harvard soon.
그는 곧 하버드를 **졸업할** 거다.

5 I have a clear m_____ of my school days.
나는 학창시절을 선명히 **기억**하고 있다.

# Campus Cleanup 교내미화

**01 cleanup** [klíːnʌp] 청소

a cleanup campaign 청소 캠페인

**02 messy** [mési] 지저분한

a messy room 지저분한 방

**03 dusty** [dʌ́sti] 먼지투성이인

a dusty road 먼지투성이 길

**04 tidy** [táidi] 깨끗한

a tidy kitchen 깨끗한 부엌

**05 post** [poust] 붙이다

post photos 사진을 붙이다

**06 wipe** [waip] 닦다

wipe off the window 창문을 닦다

**07 empty** [émpti] 비우다, 빈

empty a trash can 쓰레기통을 비우다

**08 repair** [ripέər] 고치다

repair a door 문을 고치다

**09 polish** [páliʃ] 광을 내다

polish my shoes 내 신발에 광을 내다

**10 restroom** [restruːm] (공공)화장실

clean a restroom 화장실을 청소하다

✎ 영어 단어를 완성하세요.

1   **cleanup** 청소

    →   clea [ ] up      [ ] eanup      [        ]

2   **messy** 지저분한

    →   [ ] essy      mes [ ]      [        ]

3   **dusty** 먼지투성이인

    →   dus [ ] y      d [ ] ty      [        ]

4   **tidy** 깨끗한

    →   [ ] idy      t [ ] y      [        ]

5   **post** 붙이다

    →   po [ ] t      [ ] st      [        ]

6   **wipe** 닦다

    →   [ ] ipe      w [ ] e      [        ]

7   **empty** 비우다, 빈

    →   em [ ] ty      [ ] pty      [        ]

8   **repair** 고치다

    →   repai [ ]      rep [ ] r      [        ]

9   **polish** 광을 내다

    →   polis [ ]      po [ ] sh      [        ]

10  **restroom** (공공)화장실

    →   r [ ] stroom      res [ ] oom      [        ]

# Practice

**A** 단어의 알맞은 뜻을 선으로 연결한 후, 빈칸에 단어를 직접 써보세요.

1 tidy • • 닦다 →

2 wipe • • 깨끗한 →

3 messy • • 비우다, 빈 →

4 empty • • 고치다 →

5 repair • • 지저분한 →

**B** 우리말과 일치하도록 빈칸에 알맞은 단어를 보기 에서 찾아 쓰세요.

| 보기 | post | dusty | polish | restroom | cleanup |
|---|---|---|---|---|---|

1 먼지투성이 길 → a _____ road

2 내 신발에 광을 내다 → _____ my shoes

3 청소 캠페인 → a _____ campaign

4 화장실을 청소하다 → clean a _____

5 사진을 붙이다 → _____ photos

**C** 우리말을 참고해서 빈칸에 알맞은 단어를 골라 문장을 완성하세요.

1 Let's _____ photos on the board. 사진을 그 보드판에 **붙이자**.
( post / repair )

2 I will _____ off the window. 나는 창문을 **닦을** 거다.
( wipe / polish )

3 We started a _____ campaign. 우리는 **청소** 캠페인을 시작했다.
( dusty / cleanup )

4 She is cleaning the _____. 그녀는 그 **화장실**을 청소하고 있다.
( empty / restroom )

5 They were in her _____ kitchen. 그들은 그녀의 **깨끗한** 부엌에 있었다.
( tidy / messy )

**D** 우리말을 참고해서 알맞은 단어를 넣어 문장을 완성하세요.

1 Can you r_____ the door? 너는 그 문을 **고칠** 수 있니?

2 Did you e_____ the trash can? 네가 그 쓰레기통을 **비웠니**?

3 She cleaned her m_____ room. 그녀는 자신의 **지저분한** 방을 청소했다.

4 He walked down the d_____ road. 그는 그 **먼지투성이** 길을 걸어갔다.

5 I need to p_____ my shoes with wax. 나는 신발을 왁스로 **광을 내야**겠다.

## A 다음 영어 단어의 우리말 뜻을 쓰세요.

1 basket → _____

2 proud → _____

3 forget → _____

4 happen → _____

5 during → _____

6 cleanup → _____

7 restroom → _____

8 planner → _____

9 special → _____

10 whistle → _____

11 university → _____

12 activity → _____

13 vacation → _____

14 volunteer → _____

## B 다음 우리말을 보고 영어표현을 완성하세요.

1 p_____ flowers
꽃을 꺾다

2 a t_____ kitchen
깨끗한 부엌

3 e_____ a school
학교에 입학하다

4 win a gold m_____
금메달을 따다

5 a talent c_____
장기자랑 대회

6 b_____ a shot
슛을 막다

7 p_____ photos
사진을 붙이다

8 e_____ a trash can
쓰레기통을 비우다

9 l_____ soon
곧 떠나다

10 a clear m_____
선명한 기억

11 go on a p_____
소풍을 가다

12 a m_____ room
지저분한 방

13 a big m_____
큰 경기

14 w_____ off the window
창문을 닦다

**C** 우리말과 같도록 괄호 안에서 알맞은 단어에 동그라미 하세요.

1 I want to live in the ( country / playground ). 나는 **시골**에서 살고 싶다.

2 James is the ( winner / loser ) of this game. James는 이 게임의 **승자**다.

3 He will ( enter / graduate ) from Harvard soon. 그는 곧 하버드를 **졸업할** 거다.

4 I ( forget / remember ) it clearly. 나는 그것을 확실히 **기억한다**.

5 They are ( elementary / university ) students. 그들은 **초등**학생들이다.

6 We had a ( cleanup / wonderful ) time. 우리는 **아주 멋진** 시간을 보냈다.

7 I was glad to win an ( honor / special ) prize. 나는 **우등상**을 타서 기뻤다.

8 Watching TV is my ( vacation / leisure ) activity. TV 시청이 내 **여가** 활동이다.


**D** 우리말과 같도록 다음 영어 문장을 완성하세요.

1 I w_____ for spring to come. 나는 봄이 오기를 **기다린다**.

2 This city has a large sports f_____. 이 도시에는 큰 운동 **경기장**이 있다.

3 He walked down the d_____ road. 그는 그 **먼지투성이** 길을 걸어갔다.

4 He is not a good l_____. 그는 깨끗이 승복하는 **패자**가 아니다.

5 Let's c_____ for our players! 우리 선수들을 **응원하자**!

6 I need to p_____ my shoes with wax. 나는 신발을 왁스로 **광을 내야**겠다.

7 Let's h_____ up and go home. **서둘러** 집에 가자.

8 Can you r_____ the door? 너는 그 문을 **고칠** 수 있니?

# Performances 공연

| 01 **concert** | [kánsə(:)rt] 콘서트 |
|---|---|
| give a concert 콘서트를 열다 | |

| 02 **classical** | [klǽsikəl] 클래식의 |
|---|---|
| classical music 클래식 음악 | |

| 03 **popular** | [pápjulər] 인기 있는 |
|---|---|
| popular with everyone 모두에게 인기 있는 | |

| 04 **poor** | [puər] 못하는 |
|---|---|
| poor at singing 노래를 못하는 | |

| 05 **good** | [gud] 잘하는 |
|---|---|
| good at sports 운동을 잘하는 | |

| 06 **entertain** | [entərtein] 즐겁게 하다 |
|---|---|
| entertain children 아이들을 즐겁게 하다 | |

| 07 **perform** | [pərfɔ́ːrm] 공연하다 |
|---|---|
| perform a play 연극을 공연하다 | |

| 08 **express** | [iksprés] 표현하다 |
|---|---|
| express myself 내 자신을 표현하다 | |

| 09 **imagine** | [imǽdʒin] 상상하다 |
|---|---|
| imagine a world 세상을 상상하다 | |

| 10 **audience** | [ɔ́ːdiəns] 관객 |
|---|---|
| a large audience 많은 관객 | |

✎ 영어 단어를 완성하세요.

**1** concert 콘서트

→ c ☐ ncert    co ☐ ert    ☐ ☐

**2** classical 클래식의

→ class ☐ cal    ☐ assical    ☐ ☐

**3** popular 인기 있는

→ popu ☐ ar    pop ☐ la ☐    ☐ ☐

**4** poor 못하는

→ ☐ oor    po ☐ ☐    ☐ ☐

**5** good 잘하는

→ goo ☐    ☐ o ☐ d    ☐ ☐

**6** entertain 즐겁게 하다

→ ente ☐ tain    e ☐ ter ☐ ain    ☐ ☐

**7** perform 공연하다

→ per ☐ orm    ☐ ☐ rform    ☐ ☐

**8** express 표현하다

→ expre ☐ s    ☐ press    ☐ ☐

**9** imagine 상상하다

→ ima ☐ ine    i ☐ gine    ☐ ☐

**10** audience 관객

→ au ☐ ience    ☐ dience    ☐ ☐

# Practice

**A** 단어의 알맞은 뜻을 선으로 연결한 후, 빈칸에 단어를 직접 써보세요.

1  good ·              · 인기 있는  →  [          ]

2  poor ·              · 잘하는  →  [          ]

3  popular ·           · 못하는  →  [          ]

4  express ·           · 공연하다  →  [          ]

5  perform ·           · 표현하다  →  [          ]

**B** 우리말과 일치하도록 빈칸에 알맞은 단어를 보기 에서 찾아 쓰세요.

| 보기 | concert | imagine | classical | entertain | audience |

1  클래식 음악            →  _____ music

2  콘서트를 열다          →  give a _____

3  세상을 상상하다        →  _____ a world

4  많은 관객             →  a large _____

5  아이들을 즐겁게 하다    →  _____ children

**C** 우리말을 참고해서 빈칸에 알맞은 단어를 골라 문장을 완성하세요.

1 I am _____ at singing. 나는 노래를 **못한**다.
( good / poor )

2 I _____ myself in my paintings. 나는 그림으로 내 자신을 **표현한다.**
( express / imagine )

3 She is interested in _____ music. 그녀는 **클래식** 음악에 흥미가 있다.
( concert / classical )

4 There was a large _____ at the theater. 그 극장에는 **관객**이 많았다.
( popular / audience )

5 We _____ a play at the festival. 우리는 그 페스티벌에서 연극을 **공연한다**.
( entertain / perform )

**D** 우리말을 참고해서 알맞은 단어를 넣어 문장을 완성하세요.

1 She is _g_____ at all sports.
그녀는 모든 운동을 다 **잘한**다.

2 They gave a _c_____ in London.
그들은 런던에서 **콘서트**를 열었다.

3 They _e_____ children with magic.
그들은 마술로 아이들을 **즐겁게 한다**.

4 This show is _p_____ with everyone.
이 쇼는 모두에게 **인기가 있다**.

5 Can you _i_____ a world without colors?
너는 색이 없는 세상을 **상상할** 수 있니?

# Special Days 특별한 날

**01 idea** [aidí(:)ə]
방안, 생각
have a good idea  좋은 방안이 있다

**02 decorate** [dékərèit]
장식하다
decorate a room  방을 장식하다

**03 bow** [bau]
절하다
bow to my grandparents  조부모님께 절하다

**04 traditional** [trədíʃənəl]
전통적인
traditional Korean dance  전통 한국 무용

**05 respect** [rispékt]
존경하다
respect my parents  부모님을 존경하다

**06 holiday** [hálidèi]
휴일
a national holiday  국경일(국가의 휴일)

**07 merry** [méri]
즐거운
a merry Christmas  즐거운 크리스마스

**08 touching** [tʌ́tʃiŋ]
감동적인
a touching story  감동적인 이야기

**09 impressive** [imprésiv]
인상적인
an impressive place  인상적인 장소

**10 terrific** [tərífik]
아주 멋진
look terrific  아주 멋져 보이다

✎ 영어 단어를 완성하세요.

1  idea 방안, 생각
→ ide [ ]  [ ]ea  [ ][ ]

2  decorate 장식하다
→ [ ]ecorate  de[ ]rate  [ ][ ]

3  bow 절하다
→ [ ]ow  b[ ]  [ ][ ]

4  traditional 전통적인
→ tradi[ ]ional  [ ]aditional  [ ][ ]

5  respect 존경하다
→ re[ ]pect  res[ ]ct  [ ][ ]

6  holiday 휴일
→ [ ]oliday  ho[ ]day  [ ][ ]

7  merry 즐거운
→ merr[ ]  [ ]rry  [ ][ ]

8  touching 감동적인
→ t[ ]uching  tou[ ]ing  [ ][ ]

9  impressive 인상적인
→ impressi[ ]e  im[ ]essive  [ ][ ]

10  terrific 아주 멋진
→ te[ ]rific  terri[ ]c  [ ][ ]

# Practice

**A** 단어의 알맞은 뜻을 선으로 연결한 후, 빈칸에 단어를 직접 써보세요.

| 1 | bow | • | | • | 즐거운 | → | |
| 2 | idea | • | | • | 절하다 | → | |
| 3 | merry | • | | • | 존경하다 | → | |
| 4 | respect | • | | • | 아주 멋진 | → | |
| 5 | terrific | • | | • | 방안, 생각 | → | |

**B** 우리말과 일치하도록 빈칸에 알맞은 단어를 보기 에서 찾아 쓰세요.

보기    decorate    holiday    touching    traditional    impressive

1  국경일(국가의 휴일)   →   a national _____

2  방을 장식하다   →   _____ a room

3  감동적인 이야기   →   a _____ story

4  인상적인 장소   →   an _____ place

5  전통 한국 무용   →   _____ Korean dance

**C** 우리말을 참고해서 빈칸에 알맞은 단어를 골라 문장을 완성하세요.

1 Your dress looks _____. 네 드레스가 **아주 멋져** 보인다.
( terrific / respect )

2 Tomorrow is a national _____. 내일은 국경일(국가의 **휴일**)이다.
( idea / holiday )

3 Paris was an _____ place. 파리는 **인상적인** 곳이었다.
( touching / impressive )

4 Let's _____ the room with balloons. 그 방을 풍선으로 **장식하자.**
( bow / decorate )

5 She learned _____ Korean dance. 그녀는 **전통** 한국 무용을 배웠다.
( merry / traditional )

**D** 우리말을 참고해서 알맞은 단어를 넣어 문장을 완성하세요.

1 Do you have a good  i _____ ?
너는 좋은 **방안**이 있니?

2 I wish you a  m _____ Christmas.
나는 네가 **즐거운** 크리스마스 보내길 바란다.

3 I  r _____ my parents most.
나는 부모님을 제일 **존경한다.**

4 The movie was a  t _____ story.
그 영화는 **감동적인** 이야기였다.

5 I  b _____ to my grandparents on New Year's Day.
나는 설날에 조부모님께 **절한다.**

# Jobs 직업

**01 job** [dʒɑb] 직업, 직장
get a job 직장을 구하다

**02 hire** [haiər] 고용하다
hire foreign workers 외국인 노동자를 고용하다

**03 task** [tæsk] 일, 직무
do a task 일을 하다

**04 business** [bíznis] 사업(체)
run a business 사업체를 운영하다

**05 company** [kʌ́mpəni] 회사
a computer company 컴퓨터 회사

**06 office** [ɔ́(:)fis] 사무실
open an office 사무실을 열다

**07 pilot** [páilət] 조종사
an airline pilot 비행기 조종사

**08 artist** [ɑ́ːrtist] 예술가, 아티스트
a graphic artist 그래픽 아티스트

**09 soldier** [sóuldʒər] 군인
become a soldier 군인이 되다

**10 counselor** [káunsələr] 상담사
see a counselor 상담을 받다(상담사를 보다)

영어 단어를 완성하세요.

1    job   직업, 직장

→     [ ] ob     j [ ] [ ]     [ ] [ ]

2    hire   고용하다

→     [ ] ire     h [ ] e [ ]     [ ]

3    task   일, 직무

→     tas [ ]     [ ] sk     [ ]

4    business   사업(체)

→     busi [ ] ess     bu [ ] ness     [ ] [ ]

5    company   회사

→     com [ ] any     c [ ] pany     [ ]

6    office   사무실

→     [ ] ffice     o [ ] fi [ ] e     [ ]

7    pilot   조종사

→     pi [ ] ot     p [ ] lo [ ]     [ ] [ ]

8    artist   예술가, 아티스트

→     [ ] rtist     ar [ ] [ ] st     [ ] [ ]

9    soldier   군인

→     s [ ] ldier     sol [ ] er     [ ]

10    counselor   상담사

→     counselo [ ]     c [ ] nselor     [ ] [ ]

# Practice

**A** 단어의 알맞은 뜻을 선으로 연결한 후, 빈칸에 단어를 직접 써보세요.

| | | | |
|---|---|---|---|
| 1 | job • | • 회사 | → |
| 2 | hire • | • 사무실 | → |
| 3 | task • | • 고용하다 | → |
| 4 | office • | • 일, 직무 | → |
| 5 | company • | • 직업, 직장 | → |

**B** 우리말과 일치하도록 빈칸에 알맞은 단어를 보기 에서 찾아 쓰세요.

보기     pilot     artist     soldier     counselor     business

1  사업체를 운영하다 → run a _____

2  그래픽 아티스트 → a graphic _____

3  비행기 조종사 → an airline _____

4  군인이 되다 → become a _____

5  상담을 받다(상담사를 보다) → see a _____

**C** 우리말을 참고해서 빈칸에 알맞은 단어를 골라 문장을 완성하세요.

1 He must do the _____. 그는 그 **일**을 해야만 한다.
( task / office )

2 My uncle is an airline _____. 나의 삼촌은 비행기 **조종사**다.
( pilot / artist )

3 They _____ foreign workers. 그들은 외국인 노동자들을 **고용한다**.
( job / hire )

4 My mother runs a small _____. 나의 어머니는 작은 **사업체**를 운영한다.
( soldier / business )

5 You should see a _____. 너는 상담을 받는(**상담사**를 보는) 게 좋겠다.
( company / counselor )

**D** 우리말을 참고해서 알맞은 단어를 넣어 문장을 완성하세요.

1 I want to get a j_____.
나는 **직장**을 구하고 싶다.

2 I want to be a graphic a_____.
나는 그래픽 **아티스트**가 되고 싶다.

3 We plan to open a new o_____.
우리는 새 **사무실**을 열 계획이다.

4 My dream is to become a s_____.
나의 꿈은 **군인**이 되는 거다.

5 My father works for a computer c_____.
나의 아버지는 컴퓨터 **회사**에서 일한다.

# UNIT 14

# Places 장소

| 01 **place** | [pleis] 장소, 곳 |
|---|---|
| a place to visit  방문할 곳 | |

| 02 **town** | [taun] (소)도시 |
|---|---|
| the nearest town  가장 가까운 (소)도시 | |

| 03 **village** | [vílidʒ] 마을 |
|---|---|
| a fishing village  어촌(고기 잡는 마을) | |

| 04 **located** | [loukeìtid] ~ 에 위치한 |
|---|---|
| located in Paris  파리에 위치한 | |

| 05 **hotel** | [houtél] 호텔 |
|---|---|
| stay in a hotel  호텔에 머물다 | |

| 06 **bakery** | [béikəri] 제과점 |
|---|---|
| run a bakery  제과점을 운영하다 | |

| 07 **library** | [láibrèri] 도서관 |
|---|---|
| use a library  도서관을 이용하다 | |

| 08 **bookstore** | [búkstɔ̀ːr] 서점 |
|---|---|
| an online bookstore  온라인 서점 | |

| 09 **airport** | [ɛ́ərpɔ̀ːrt] 공항 |
|---|---|
| arrive at the airport  공항에 도착하다 | |

| 10 **station** | [stéiʃən] 역 |
|---|---|
| a subway station  지하철역 | |

영어 단어를 완성하세요.

**1** place 장소, 곳

→ ☐ lace  p ☐ a ☐ e  ☐ ☐

**2** town (소)도시

→ tow ☐  t ☐ ☐ n  ☐ ☐

**3** village 마을

→ ☐ illage  villa ☐ ☐  ☐ ☐

**4** located ~에 위치한

→ locate ☐  lo ☐ ☐ ted  ☐ ☐

**5** hotel 호텔

→ ☐ otel  h ☐ ☐ el  ☐ ☐

**6** bakery 제과점

→ ☐ akery  ba ☐ er ☐  ☐ ☐

**7** library 도서관

→ li ☐ rary  l ☐ br ☐ ry  ☐ ☐

**8** bookstore 서점

→ boo ☐ store  b ☐ oksto ☐ e  ☐ ☐

**9** airport 공항

→ air ☐ ort  ☐ ☐ rport  ☐ ☐

**10** station 역

→ s ☐ ation  st ☐ ti ☐ n  ☐ ☐

# Practice

**A** 단어의 알맞은 뜻을 선으로 연결한 후, 빈칸에 단어를 직접 써보세요.

1  place  •            •  호텔        →  [_____]

2  hotel  •            •  서점        →  [_____]

3  bakery  •           •  도서관      →  [_____]

4  library  •          •  제과점      →  [_____]

5  bookstore  •        •  장소, 곳    →  [_____]

**B** 우리말과 일치하도록 빈칸에 알맞은 단어를 보기 에서 찾아 쓰세요.

| 보기 | town | village | airport | station | located |
|------|------|---------|---------|---------|---------|

1  어촌(고기 잡는 마을)  →  a fishing _____

2  지하철역  →  a subway _____

3  가장 가까운 (소)도시  →  the nearest _____

4  파리에 위치한  →  _____ in Paris

5  공항에 도착하다  →  arrive at the _____

**C** 우리말을 참고해서 빈칸에 알맞은 단어를 골라 문장을 완성하세요.

1 This was a little fishing _____. 이곳은 작은 어촌(고기 잡는 **마을**)이었다.
( town / village )

2 The office is _____ in Paris. 그 사무실은 파리에 **위치해** 있다.
( located / place )

3 He created this online _____. 그는 이 온라인 **서점**을 만들었다.
( hotel / bookstore )

4 How can I get to the subway _____? 그 지하철**역**에는 어떻게 가야 하니?
( airport / station )

5 He runs a French _____ in Seoul. 그는 서울에서 프랑스 **제과점**을 운영한다.
( bakery / library )

**D** 우리말을 참고해서 알맞은 단어를 넣어 문장을 완성하세요.

1 He stayed in a  h_____ last night.
그는 지난밤에 **호텔**에 머물렀다.

2 He walked to the nearest  t_____.
그는 가장 가까운 **(소)도시**로 걸어갔다.

3 Seoul is a nice  p_____ to visit.
서울은 방문하기에 좋은 **곳**이다.

4 What time did you arrive at the  a_____?
너는 몇 시에 **공항**에 도착했니?

5 You can use the  l_____ after school.
여러분은 방과후 그 **도서관**을 이용할 수 있다.

# Cities & Nations 도시와 나라

| 01 **nation** [néiʃən] 국가 |
| --- |
| Asian nations 아시아 국가들 |

| 02 **capital** [kǽpitəl] 수도 |
| --- |
| the capital of Korea 한국의 수도 |

| 03 **abroad** [əbrɔ́ːd] 해외에 |
| --- |
| go abroad 해외에 가다 |

| 04 **building** [bíldiŋ] 건물 |
| --- |
| a tall building 고층 건물 |

| 05 **crowded** [kráudid] 붐비는 |
| --- |
| be so crowded 엄청 붐비다 |

| 06 **busy** [bízi] 복잡한, 바쁜 |
| --- |
| a busy road 복잡한 도로 |

| 07 **metropolis** [mətrápəlis] 대도시 |
| --- |
| a modern metropolis 현대적 대도시 |

| 08 **outskirt** [áutskəːrt] 변두리, 교외 |
| --- |
| the outskirt of London 런던의 변두리 |

| 09 **facility** [fəsíləti] 시설 |
| --- |
| a medical facility 의료 시설 |

| 10 **local** [lóukəl] 지역[현지]의 |
| --- |
| a local school 지역 학교 |

✎ 영어 단어를 완성하세요.

1  **nation** 국가
→ nati _ n  |  na _ on  |  ___ ___

2  **capital** 수도
→ _ apital  |  ca _ tal  |  ___ ___

3  **abroad** 해외에
→ abroa _  |  _ road  |  ___ ___

4  **building** 건물
→ _ uilding  |  b _ lding  |  ___ ___

5  **crowded** 붐비는
→ c _ owded  |  cr _ ded  |  ___ ___

6  **busy** 복잡한, 바쁜
→ bu _ y  |  _ sy  |  ___ ___

7  **metropolis** 대도시
→ metr _ polis  |  me _ opolis  |  ___ ___

8  **outskirt** 변두리, 교외
→ o _ tskirt  |  out _ irt  |  ___ ___

9  **facility** 시설
→ _ acility  |  fa _ lity  |  ___ ___

10  **local** 지역[현지]의
→ loca _  |  l _ al  |  ___ ___

# Practice

**A** 단어의 알맞은 뜻을 선으로 연결한 후, 빈칸에 단어를 직접 써보세요.

1  busy  •          •  건물        →
2  nation  •        •  수도        →
3  abroad  •        •  국가        →
4  capital  •       •  해외에       →
5  building  •      •  복잡한, 바쁜   →

**B** 우리말과 일치하도록 빈칸에 알맞은 단어를 보기 에서 찾아 쓰세요.

보기    local    crowded    outskirt    facility    metropolis

1  지역 학교        →   a _____ school

2  의료 시설        →   a medical _____

3  엄청 붐비다       →   be so _____

4  현대적 대도시      →   a modern _____

5  런던의 변두리      →   the _____ of London

**C** 우리말을 참고해서 빈칸에 알맞은 단어를 골라 문장을 완성하세요.

1 China is one of the Asian _____. 중국은 아시아 **국가들** 중의 하나다.
( nations / capitals )

2 She works in a medical _____. 그녀는 의료 **시설**에서 일한다.
( local / facility )

3 The street was so _____ today. 오늘 그 거리가 엄청 **붐볐다**.
( abroad / crowded )

4 Do you see the tall _____ over there? 너는 저기 고층 **건물**이 보이니?
( building / metropolis )

5 We reached the _____ of London. 우리는 런던의 **변두리**에 도착했다.
( busy / outskirt )

**D** 우리말을 참고해서 알맞은 단어를 넣어 문장을 완성하세요.

1 Tom goes to the l_____ school. Tom은 그 **지역** 학교에 다닌다.

2 My house is on a very b_____ road. 나의 집은 아주 **복잡한** 도로에 있다.

3 I hope to go a_____ next year. 나는 내년에 **해외에** 가고 싶다.

4 Seoul is the c_____ of Korea. 서울은 한국의 **수도**다.

5 New York is a modern m_____. 뉴욕은 현대적 **대도시**다.

## A  다음 영어 단어의 우리말 뜻을 쓰세요.

1  nation  →  _____

2  imagine  →  _____

3  airport  →  _____

4  entertain  →  _____

5  library  →  _____

6  bookstore  →  _____

7  holiday  →  _____

8  company  →  _____

9  popular  →  _____

10  counselor  →  _____

11  perform  →  _____

12  facility  →  _____

13  respect  →  _____

14  impressive  →  _____

## B  다음 우리말을 보고 영어표현을 완성하세요.

1  get a  j_____
직장을 구하다

2  do a  t_____
일을 하다

3  have a good  i_____
좋은 방안이 있다

4  an airline  p_____
비행기 조종사

5  stay in a  h_____
호텔에 머물다

6  the nearest  t_____
가장 가까운 (소)도시

7  a  b_____  road
복잡한 도로

8  b_____  to my grandparents
조부모님께 절하다

9  h_____  foreign workers
외국인 노동자를 고용하다

10  go  a_____
해외에 가다

11  give a  c_____
콘서트를 열다

12  run a  b_____
제과점을 운영하다

13  a  p_____  to visit
방문할 곳

14  a tall  b_____
고층 건물

**C** 우리말과 같도록 괄호 안에서 알맞은 단어에 동그라미 하세요.

1  I am ( poor / good ) at singing.  나는 노래를 **못한**다.

2  My dream is to become a ( soldier / counselor ).  나의 꿈은 **군인**이 되는 거다.

3  My mother runs a small ( building / business ).  나의 어머니는 작은 **사업체**를 운영한다.

4  How can I get to the subway ( airport / station )?  그 지하철**역**에는 어떻게 가야 하니?

5  The office is ( crowded / located ) in Paris.  그 사무실은 파리에 **위치해** 있다.

6  Let's ( decorate / express ) the room with balloons.  그 방을 풍선으로 **장식하**자.

7  The movie was a ( classical / touching ) story.  그 영화는 **감동적인** 이야기였다.

8  She learned ( terrific / traditional ) Korean dance.  그녀는 **전통** 한국 무용을 배웠다.

**D** 우리말과 같도록 다음 영어 문장을 완성하세요.

1  She is  g_____  at all sports.  그녀는 모든 운동을 다 **잘한**다.

2  Tom goes to the  l_____  school.  Tom은 그 **지역** 학교에 다닌다.

3  I wish you a  m_____  Christmas.  나는 네가 **즐거운** 크리스마스 보내길 바란다.

4  We plan to open a new  o_____.  우리는 새 **사무실**을 열 계획이다.

5  This was a little fishing  v_____.  이곳은 작은 어촌(고기 잡는 **마을**)이었다.

6  The street was so  c_____  today.  오늘 그 거리가 엄청 **붐볐**다.

7  Seoul is the  c_____  of Korea.  서울은 한국의 **수도**다.

8  I  e_____  myself in my paintings.  나는 그림으로 내 자신을 **표현한**다.

# World 세계

| 01 | **world** | [wəːrld] 세계, 세상 |
|---|---|---|
| | in the world 세상에서 | |

| 02 | **global** | [glóubəl] 지구의 |
|---|---|---|
| | global warming 지구 온난화 | |

| 03 | **peace** | [piːs] 평화 |
|---|---|---|
| | in peace 평화롭게 | |

| 04 | **war** | [wɔːr] 전쟁 |
|---|---|---|
| | during the war 전쟁 중에 | |

| 05 | **island** | [áilənd] 섬 |
|---|---|---|
| | an island country 섬나라 | |

| 06 | **continent** | [kántənənt] 대륙 |
|---|---|---|
| | the African continent 아프리카 대륙 | |

| 07 | **polar** | [póulər] 북극[남극]의 |
|---|---|---|
| | a polar bear 북극곰 | |

| 08 | **human** | [hjuːmən] 인간[인류]의 |
|---|---|---|
| | in human history 인류역사에서 | |

| 09 | **iceberg** | [áisbəːrg] 빙산 |
|---|---|---|
| | hit an iceberg 빙산에 부딪치다 | |

| 10 | **erupt** | [irʌ́pt] 분출하다 |
|---|---|---|
| | erupt from a volcano 화산에서 분출하다 | |

✎ 영어 단어를 완성하세요.

1 **world** 세계, 세상

→ [ ]orld      wor[ ]      [ ][ ]

2 **global** 지구의

→ glo[ ]al      [ ]obal      [ ][ ]

3 **peace** 평화

→ [ ]eace      p[ ]ce      [ ][ ]

4 **war** 전쟁

→ wa[ ]      [ ]r      [ ][ ]

5 **island** 섬

→ isla[ ]d      [ ]land      [ ][ ]

6 **continent** 대륙

→ [ ]ontinent      con[ ]nent      [ ][ ]

7 **polar** 북극[남극]의

→ p[ ]lar      pol[ ]      [ ][ ]

8 **human** 인간[인류]의

→ h[ ]man      hu[ ]a[ ]      [ ][ ]

9 **iceberg** 빙산

→ i[ ]eberg      icebe[ ]      [ ][ ]

10 **erupt** 분출하다

→ e[ ]upt      er[ ]t      [ ][ ]

# Practice

**A**  단어의 알맞은 뜻을 선으로 연결한 후, 빈칸에 단어를 직접 써보세요.

1  war  •  • 평화  →
2  world  •  • 전쟁  →
3  human  •  • 빙산  →
4  peace  •  • 인간 [인류]의  →
5  iceberg  •  • 세계, 세상  →

**B**  우리말과 일치하도록 빈칸에 알맞은 단어를 보기 에서 찾아 쓰세요.

| 보기 | erupt | global | polar | island | continent |

1  북극곰  →  a _____ bear

2  섬나라  →  an _____ country

3  화산에서 분출하다  →  _____ from a volcano

4  지구 온난화  →  _____ warming

5  아프리카 대륙  →  the African _____

**C**  우리말을 참고해서 빈칸에 알맞은 단어를 골라 문장을 완성하세요.

1  Many people died during the _____.  많은 사람들이 **전쟁** 중에 죽었다.
    ( war / peace )

2  Japan is an _____ country.  일본은 **섬**나라다.
    ( human / island )

3  Ash _____ from the volcano.  화산재가 그 화산에서 **분출했다**.
    ( erupted / iceberg )

4  A _____ bear lives near the North Pole.  **북극**곰은 북극 근처에 산다.
    ( polar / continent )

5  We have to stop _____ warming.  우리는 **지구** 온난화를 막아야 한다.
    ( world / global )

**D**  우리말을 참고해서 알맞은 단어를 넣어 문장을 완성하세요.

1  It is the largest animal in  h_____  history.
    그것은 **인류**역사에서 가장 큰 동물이다.

2  I wish we can all live in  p_____ .
    나는 우리 모두 **평화**롭게 살 수 있으면 좋겠다.

3  He crossed the African  c_____ .
    그는 아프리카 **대륙**을 횡단했다.

4  The Titanic hit the  i_____ in the ocean.
    타이타닉은 바다의 **빙산**에 부딪쳤다.

5  The Nile is the longest river in the  w_____ .
    나일강은 **세상**에서 제일 긴 강이다.

# Marriage 결혼

| 01 | **marry** | [mǽri] 결혼하다 |
|---|---|---|
| | marry her   그녀와 결혼하다 | |

| 02 | **date** | [deit] 데이트 |
|---|---|---|
| | have a date   데이트가 있다 | |

| 03 | **single** | [síŋgl] 미혼[혼자]의 |
|---|---|---|
| | be single   미혼이다 | |

| 04 | **couple** | [kʌ́pl] 부부, 한 쌍 |
|---|---|---|
| | a young couple   젊은 부부 | |

| 05 | **wedding** | [wédiŋ] 결혼식 |
|---|---|---|
| | attend a wedding   결혼식에 참석하다 | |

| 06 | **divorce** | [divɔ́ːrs] 이혼 |
|---|---|---|
| | get a divorce   이혼하다 | |

| 07 | **propose** | [prəpóuz] 청혼하다 |
|---|---|---|
| | propose to her   그녀에게 청혼하다 | |

| 08 | **bride** | [braid] 신부 |
|---|---|---|
| | a new bride   새 신부 | |

| 09 | **groom** | [grum] 신랑 |
|---|---|---|
| | friends of the groom   신랑의 친구들 | |

| 10 | **honeymoon** | [hʌ́nimùːn] 신혼여행 |
|---|---|---|
| | on their honeymoon   그들의 신혼여행으로 | |

✎ 영어 단어를 완성하세요.

**1** marry 결혼하다

→ ☐arry　　mar☐　　☐☐ ☐☐

**2** date 데이트

→ d☐te　　da☐　　☐☐ ☐☐

**3** single 미혼[혼자]의

→ sin☐le　　si☐g☐e　　☐☐

**4** couple 부부, 한쌍

→ cou☐le　　c☐ple　　☐☐ ☐☐

**5** wedding 결혼식

→ we☐ding　　weddi☐　　☐☐ ☐☐

**6** divorce 이혼

→ div☐rce　　d☐orce　　☐☐ ☐☐

**7** propose 청혼하다

→ p☐opose　　pro☐o☐e　　☐☐ ☐☐

**8** bride 신부

→ ☐ride　　br☐☐e　　☐☐ ☐☐

**9** groom 신랑

→ ☐room　　gro☐☐　　☐☐ ☐☐

**10** honeymoon 신혼여행

→ ho☐eymoon　　hon☐☐moon　　☐☐ ☐☐

# Practice

**A** 단어의 알맞은 뜻을 선으로 연결한 후, 빈칸에 단어를 직접 써보세요.

1 bride •　　　　　•　이혼 ⟶ _____

2 marry •　　　　　•　신랑 ⟶ _____

3 groom •　　　　　•　신부 ⟶ _____

4 divorce •　　　　　•　청혼하다 ⟶ _____

5 propose •　　　　　•　결혼하다 ⟶ _____

**B** 우리말과 일치하도록 빈칸에 알맞은 단어를 보기 에서 찾아 쓰세요.

보기　　date　　single　　couple　　wedding　　honeymoon

1 미혼이다 ⟶ be _____

2 젊은 부부 ⟶ a young _____

3 데이트가 있다 ⟶ have a _____

4 결혼식에 참석하다 ⟶ attend a _____

5 그들의 신혼여행으로 ⟶ on their _____

**C** 우리말을 참고해서 빈칸에 알맞은 단어를 골라 문장을 완성하세요.

1 My uncle is _____. 나의 삼촌은 **미혼이**다.
( single / couple )

2 I have a _____ with Sarah. 나는 Sarah와 **데이트**가 있다.
( date / wedding )

3 Paul wants to _____ her. Paul은 그녀와 **결혼하기를** 원한다.
( marry / divorce )

4 They are friends of the _____. 그들은 **신랑**의 친구들이다.
( bride / groom )

5 Her boyfriend _____ to her. 그녀의 남자친구는 그녀에게 **청혼했다**.
( proposed / honeymoon )


**D** 우리말을 참고해서 알맞은 단어를 넣어 문장을 완성하세요.

1 They are getting a d_____.
그들은 **이혼**하려고 한다.

2 Mr. White introduced his new b_____.
White 씨는 그의 새 **신부**를 소개했다.

3 Many people attended the w_____.
많은 사람들이 그 **결혼식**에 참석했다.

4 They went to Italy on their h_____.
그들은 **신혼여행**으로 이탈리아에 갔다.

5 The young c_____ moved into a new house.
그 젊은 **부부**는 새 집으로 이사했다.

# Environment 환경

| 01 | **environment** | [inváiərənmənt] 환경 |
|---|---|---|
| | bad for the environment 환경에 나쁜 | |

| 02 | **issue** | [íʃuː] 쟁점, 문제 |
|---|---|---|
| | a key issue 핵심 쟁점 | |

| 03 | **plastic** | [plǽstik] 플라스틱[비닐](의) |
|---|---|---|
| | a plastic bag 비닐봉지 | |

| 04 | **paper** | [péipər] 종이 |
|---|---|---|
| | a piece of paper 종이 한 장 | |

| 05 | **dump** | [dʌmp] 버리다 |
|---|---|---|
| | dump waste 폐기물을 버리다 | |

| 06 | **protect** | [prətékt] 보호하다 |
|---|---|---|
| | protect nature 자연을 보호하다 | |

| 07 | **recycle** | [riːsáikl] 재활용하다 |
|---|---|---|
| | recycle bottles 병을 재활용하다 | |

| 08 | **destroy** | [distrɔ́i] 파괴하다 |
|---|---|---|
| | destroy a city 도시를 파괴하다 | |

| 09 | **harm** | [hɑːrm] 해, 해악 |
|---|---|---|
| | do harm 해를 끼치다 | |

| 10 | **pollution** | [pəljúːʃən] 오염 |
|---|---|---|
| | air pollution 대기 오염 | |

✎ 영어 단어를 완성하세요.

**1** environment 환경

→ ☐nvironment  en☐iron☐ent  ☐ ☐

**2** issue 쟁점, 문제

→ i☐sue  iss☐  ☐ ☐

**3** plastic 플라스틱[비닐] (의)

→ p☐astic  ☐lasti☐  ☐ ☐

**4** paper 종이

→ pape☐  p☐er  ☐ ☐

**5** dump 버리다

→ dum☐  ☐u☐p  ☐ ☐

**6** protect 보호하다

→ p☐otect  pr☐te☐t  ☐ ☐

**7** recycle 재활용하다

→ ☐ecycle  re☐cle  ☐ ☐

**8** destroy 파괴하다

→ destro☐  d☐str☐y  ☐ ☐

**9** harm 해, 해악

→ ☐arm  h☐r☐  ☐ ☐

**10** pollution 오염

→ pollu☐ion  pol☐☐tion  ☐ ☐

# Practice

**A** 단어의 알맞은 뜻을 선으로 연결한 후, 빈칸에 단어를 직접 써보세요.

| 1 | dump | • | • | 종이 | → | |
| 2 | paper | • | • | 버리다 | → | |
| 3 | destroy | • | • | 보호하다 | → | |
| 4 | protect | • | • | 파괴하다 | → | |
| 5 | recycle | • | • | 재활용하다 | → | |

**B** 우리말과 일치하도록 빈칸에 알맞은 단어를 보기 에서 찾아 쓰세요.

보기　　harm　　issue　　plastic　　pollution　　environment

1 핵심 쟁점 　　→　　a key ＿＿＿＿＿＿＿

2 비닐봉지 　　→　　a ＿＿＿＿＿＿＿ bag

3 대기 오염 　　→　　air ＿＿＿＿＿＿＿

4 해를 끼치다 　　→　　do ＿＿＿＿＿＿＿

5 환경에 나쁜 　　→　　bad for the ＿＿＿＿＿＿＿

**C** 우리말을 참고해서 빈칸에 알맞은 단어를 골라 문장을 완성하세요.

1 The key _____ is cost. 그 핵심 **쟁점**은 비용이다.
( harm / issue )

2 Do you have a _____ bag? 너는 **비닐봉지**가 있니?
( paper / plastic )

3 The factory _____ waste into the river. 그 공장은 폐기물을 그 강에 **버렸다**.
( dumped / recycled )

4 The war completely _____ the city. 그 전쟁은 그 도시를 완전히 **파괴했다**.
( destroyed / protected )

5 Air _____ in Seoul is serious. 서울의 대기 **오염**은 심각하다.
( pollution / environment )

**D** 우리말을 참고해서 알맞은 단어를 넣어 문장을 완성하세요.

1 We should p_____ nature.
우리는 자연을 **보호해야** 한다.

2 We r_____ bottles and newspaper.
우리는 병과 신문을 **재활용한다**.

3 Can I have another piece of p_____?
내가 **종이** 한 장 더 써도 되니?

4 These are bad for the e_____.
이것들은 **환경**에 나쁘다.

5 Smoking can do h_____ to your health.
흡연은 네 건강에 **해**를 끼칠 수 있다.

# Disasters 재해

**01 accident** [ǽksidənt] 사고
have an accident 사고를 당하다

**02 result** [rizʌ́lt] 결과
as a result 결과적으로

**03 terrible** [térəbl] 끔찍한
terrible news 끔찍한 소식

**04 lucky** [lʌ́ki] 운이 좋은
be lucky to survive 운 좋게 살아남다

**05 flood** [flʌd] 홍수, 범람
be in flood 범람하다

**06 earthquake** [ə́ːrθkwèik] 지진
a powerful earthquake 강력한 지진

**07 fall** [fɔːl] 떨어지다
fall down stairs 계단에서 떨어지다

**08 cause** [kɔːz] 일으키다
cause flooding 홍수를 일으키다

**09 crash** [kræʃ] 충돌하다
crash into a tree 나무에 충돌하다

**10 suffer** [sʌ́fər] 고생하다
suffer from allergies 알레르기로 고생하다

✎ 영어 단어를 완성하세요.

1 accident 사고
→ a ☐ cident    acc ☐ de ☐ t    ☐ ☐

2 result 결과
→ ☐ esult    re ☐ lt    ☐ ☐

3 terrible 끔찍한
→ terri ☐ le    t ☐ r ☐ ible    ☐ ☐

4 lucky 운이 좋은
→ ☐ ucky    l ☐ c ☐ y    ☐ ☐

5 flood 홍수, 범람
→ ☐ lood    f ☐ o ☐ d    ☐ ☐

6 earthquake 지진
→ earth ☐ uake    ear ☐ ☐ quake    ☐ ☐

7 fall 떨어지다
→ f ☐ ll    ☐ a ☐ l    ☐ ☐

8 cause 일으키다
→ ☐ ause    c ☐ ☐ se    ☐ ☐

9 crash 충돌하다
→ cra ☐ h    c ☐ as ☐    ☐ ☐

10 suffer 고생하다
→ ☐ uffer    s ☐ ☐ fer    ☐ ☐

# Practice

**A** 단어의 알맞은 뜻을 선으로 연결한 후, 빈칸에 단어를 직접 써보세요.

| | | | |
|---|---|---|---|
| 1 | lucky • | • 결과 | → _____ |
| 2 | suffer • | • 홍수, 범람 | → _____ |
| 3 | result • | • 끔찍한 | → _____ |
| 4 | flood • | • 운이 좋은 | → _____ |
| 5 | terrible • | • 고생하다 | → _____ |

**B** 우리말과 일치하도록 빈칸에 알맞은 단어를 보기 에서 찾아 쓰세요.

| 보기 | accident | cause | fall | crash | earthquake |
|---|---|---|---|---|---|

1 계단에서 떨어지다   →   _____ down stairs

2 나무에 충돌하다   →   _____ into a tree

3 홍수를 일으키다   →   _____ flooding

4 사고를 당하다   →   have an _____

5 강력한 지진   →   a powerful _____

**C** 우리말을 참고해서 빈칸에 알맞은 단어를 골라 문장을 완성하세요.

1 I got some _____ news. 나는 **끔찍한** 소식을 들었다.
( lucky / terrible )

2 The truck _____ into a tree. 그 트럭은 나무에 **충돌했다.**
( crashed / suffered )

3 The river is in _____. 그 강은 **범람**하고 있다.
( fall / flood )

4 As a _____, she is in the hospital. **결과적으로,** 그녀는 병원에 입원해 있다.
( result / cause )

5 He had an _____ on the road. 그는 그 도로에서 **사고**를 당했다.
( accident / earthquake )


**D** 우리말을 참고해서 알맞은 단어를 넣어 문장을 완성하세요.

1 I didn't f _____ down stairs.
나는 계단에서 **떨어지지** 않았다.

2 He was l _____ to survive the fire.
그는 **운 좋게** 그 화재에서 살아남았다.

3 I s _____ from allergies in spring.
나는 봄에 알레르기로 **고생한다.**

4 The heavy rain c _____ d flooding.
그 폭우가 홍수를 **일으켰다.**

5 A powerful e _____ hit Tokyo.
강력한 **지진**이 도쿄를 강타했다.

# Religion 종교

| | |
|---|---|
| **01 pray** [prei] 기도[기원]하다<br>pray for peace 평화를 기원하다 | **02 temple** [témpl] 사원, 절<br>go to temple 절에 다니다 |
| **03 god** [gad] 신<br>Greek gods 그리스 신들 | **04 sin** [sin] 죄, 죄악<br>commit a sin 죄를 짓다 |
| **05 forgive** [fərgív] 용서하다<br>forgive and forget 용서하고 잊다 | **06 believe** [bilíːv] 믿다<br>believe in God 하느님을 믿다 |
| **07 life** [laif] 삶, 생명<br>save her life 그녀의 생명을 구하다 | **08 death** [deθ] 죽음<br>escape death 죽음을 면하다 |
| **09 create** [kriéit] 창조하다<br>create the world 세상을 창조하다 | **10 religion** [rilídʒən] 종교<br>different religions 다른 종교들 |

영어 단어를 완성하세요.

1 **pray** 기도[기원]하다

→ p ☐ ay   pr ☐ ☐   ☐☐ | ☐☐

2 **temple** 사원, 절

→ tem ☐ le   te ☐ p ☐ e   ☐☐ | ☐☐

3 **god** 신

→ g ☐ d   ☐ o ☐   ☐☐ | ☐☐

4 **sin** 죄, 죄악

→ ☐ in   s ☐ ☐   ☐☐ | ☐☐

5 **forgive** 용서하다

→ ☐ orgive   f ☐ rg ☐ ve   ☐☐ | ☐☐

6 **believe** 믿다

→ bel ☐ eve   ☐ elie ☐ e   ☐☐ | ☐☐

7 **life** 삶, 생명

→ li ☐ e   l ☐ f ☐   ☐☐ | ☐☐

8 **death** 죽음

→ dea ☐ h   d ☐ ☐ th   ☐☐

9 **create** 창조하다

→ ☐ reate   c ☐ ea ☐ e   ☐☐ | ☐☐

10 **religion** 종교

→ reli ☐ ion   re ☐ ☐ gion   ☐☐ | ☐☐

# Practice

**A** 단어의 알맞은 뜻을 선으로 연결한 후, 빈칸에 단어를 직접 써보세요.

| 1 | sin | • | • | 신 | → | |
| 2 | god | • | • | 죽음 | → | |
| 3 | life | • | • | 사원, 절 | → | |
| 4 | death | • | • | 삶, 생명 | → | |
| 5 | temple | • | • | 죄, 죄악 | → | |

**B** 우리말과 일치하도록 빈칸에 알맞은 단어를 보기 에서 찾아 쓰세요.

보기      religion      create      pray      believe      forgive

| 1 | 평화를 기원하다 | → | _____ for peace |
| 2 | 하느님을 믿다 | → | _____ in God |
| 3 | 용서하고 잊다 | → | _____ and forget |
| 4 | 세상을 창조하다 | → | _____ the world |
| 5 | 다른 종교들 | → | different _____ s |

**C** 우리말을 참고해서 빈칸에 알맞은 단어를 골라 문장을 완성하세요.

1 Zeus is the king of Greek _____. Zeus는 그리스 **신들**의 왕이다.
( gods / sins )

2 We go to _____ on Saturdays. 우리는 토요일마다 **절**에 간다.
( pray / temple )

3 It's hard to _____ and forget. **용서하고** 잊는 것은 어렵다.
( create / forgive )

4 He barely escaped _____. 그는 간신히 **죽음**을 면했다.
( life / death )

5 Each country has different _____. 나라마다 다른 **종교들**이 있다.
( believes / religions )


**D** 우리말을 참고해서 알맞은 단어를 넣어 문장을 완성하세요.

1 Let's p_____ for peace. 평화를 위해 **기도하자**.

2 He committed the s_____ of murder. 그는 살인**죄**를 저질렀다.

3 Do you b_____ in God? 너는 하느님을 **믿니**?

4 The firefighter saved her l_____. 그 소방관은 그녀의 **생명**을 구했다.

5 God c_____d the world in six days. 하느님은 6일만에 세상을 **창조했다**.

## A 다음 영어 단어의 우리말 뜻을 쓰세요.

1 island → _____

2 groom → _____

3 peace → _____

4 death → _____

5 result → _____

6 forgive → _____

7 create → _____

8 believe → _____

9 destroy → _____

10 accident → _____

11 iceberg → _____

12 pollution → _____

13 earthquake → _____

14 environment → _____

## B 다음 우리말을 보고 영어표현을 완성하세요.

1 have a  d _____
데이트가 있다

2 during the  w _____
전쟁 중에

3 do  h _____
해를 끼치다

4  d _____ waste
폐기물을 버리다

5  f _____ down stairs
계단에서 떨어지다

6  p _____ for peace
평화를 기원하다

7 a new  b _____
새 신부

8 in the  w _____
세상에서

9 a  p _____ bear
북극곰

10 a piece of  p _____
종이 한 장

11 be  s _____
미혼이다

12  e _____ from a volcano
화산에서 분출하다

13 a young  c _____
젊은 부부

14 go to  t _____
절에 다니다

**C** 우리말과 같도록 괄호 안에서 알맞은 단어에 동그라미 하세요.

1 Zeus is the king of Greek ( gods / wars ). Zeus는 그리스 **신들**의 왕이다.

2 I got some ( lucky / terrible ) news. 나는 **끔찍한** 소식을 들었다.

3 We have to stop ( world / global ) warming. 우리는 **지구** 온난화를 막아야 한다.

4 Do you have a ( paper / plastic ) bag? 너는 **비닐봉지**가 있니?

5 We ( recycle / protect ) bottles and newspaper. 우리는 병과 신문을 **재활용한다**.

6 They are getting a ( divorce / wedding ). 그들은 **이혼**하려고 한다.

7 He crossed the African ( island / continent ). 그는 아프리카 **대륙**을 횡단했다.

8 The heavy rain ( caused / crashed ) flooding. 그 폭우가 홍수를 **일으켰다**.

**D** 우리말과 같도록 다음 영어 문장을 완성하세요.

1 The firefighter saved her l_____. 그 소방관은 그녀의 **생명**을 구했다.

2 He committed the s_____ of murder. 그는 살인**죄**를 저질렀다.

3 Paul wants to m_____ her. Paul은 그녀와 **결혼하기를** 원한다.

4 The key i_____ is cost. 그 핵심 **쟁점**은 비용이다.

5 The river is in f_____. 그 강은 **범람**하고 있다.

6 We should p_____ nature. 우리는 자연을 **보호해야** 한다.

7 He was l_____ to survive the fire. 그는 **운 좋게** 그 화재에서 살아남았다.

8 I s_____ from allergies in spring. 나는 봄에 알레르기로 **고생한다**.

# Animals 동물

| 01 | **animal** | [ǽnəməl]<br>동물 |
|---|---|---|
| | wild animals  야생 동물들 | |

| 02 | **prey** | [prei]<br>먹이[사냥감] |
|---|---|---|
| | easy prey  쉬운 먹이 | |

| 03 | **raise** | [reiz]<br>기르다, 재배하다 |
|---|---|---|
| | raise chickens  닭을 기르다 | |

| 04 | **wild** | [waild]<br>야생(의) |
|---|---|---|
| | in the wild  야생에서 | |

| 05 | **domestic** | [dəméstik]<br>(동물이) 사육되는 |
|---|---|---|
| | domestic animals  가축(사육되는 동물들) | |

| 06 | **feed** | [fi:d]<br>먹이를 주다 |
|---|---|---|
| | feed a dog  개에게 먹이를 주다 | |

| 07 | **beast** | [bi:st]<br>짐승 |
|---|---|---|
| | neither bird nor beast  새도 짐승도 아닌 | |

| 08 | **live** | [liv]<br>살다 |
|---|---|---|
| | live in a cave  동굴에서 살다 | |

| 09 | **kingdom** | [kíŋdəm]<br>왕국 |
|---|---|---|
| | the animal kingdom  동물의 왕국 | |

| 10 | **species** | [spí:ʃi:z]<br>종류, (생물) 종 |
|---|---|---|
| | endangered species  멸종 위기 종 | |

✎ 영어 단어를 완성하세요.

1 animal 동물

→ ☐ nimal    an ☐ m ☐ l    ☐ ☐

2 prey 먹이[사냥감]

→ p ☐ ey    ☐ r ☐ y    ☐ ☐

3 raise 기르다, 재배하다

→ ☐ aise    r ☐ i ☐ e    ☐ ☐

4 wild 야생(의)

→ wil ☐    ☐ i ☐ d    ☐ ☐

5 domestic (동물이) 사육되는

→ do ☐ estic    ☐ omes ☐ ic    ☐ ☐

6 feed 먹이를 주다

→ f ☐ ed    ☐ ee ☐    ☐ ☐

7 beast 짐승

→ ☐ east    b ☐ st    ☐ ☐

8 live 살다

→ l ☐ ve    ☐ i ☐ e    ☐ ☐

9 kingdom 왕국

→ kin ☐ dom    ☐ ing ☐ om    ☐ ☐

10 species 종류, (생물) 종

→ s ☐ ecies    spe ☐ i ☐ s    ☐ ☐

# Practice

**A** 단어의 알맞은 뜻을 선으로 연결한 후, 빈칸에 단어를 직접 써보세요.

| 1 | animal | • | • | 먹이 [사냥감] | → | |
| 2 | prey | • | • | 왕국 | → | |
| 3 | wild | • | • | 동물 | → | |
| 4 | live | • | • | 야생(의) | → | |
| 5 | kingdom | • | • | 살다 | → | |

**B** 우리말과 일치하도록 빈칸에 알맞은 단어를 보기 에서 찾아 쓰세요.

보기    raise    domestic    feed    beast    species

1 닭을 기르다 → _____ chickens

2 멸종 위기 종 → endangered _____

3 개에게 먹이를 주다 → _____ a dog

4 새도 짐승도 아닌 → neither bird nor _____

5 가축(사육되는 동물들) → _____ animals

**C** 우리말을 참고해서 빈칸에 알맞은 단어를 골라 문장을 완성하세요.

1 Some wild _____ are in the forest. 몇몇 야생 **동물들**이 그 숲 속에 있다.
( animals / beasts )

2 What do you _____ the dog? 너는 그 개에게 무엇을 **먹이로 주니**?
( feed / live )

3 People rear _____ animals. 사람들은 가축(**사육되는** 동물)들을 기른다.
( domestic / kingdom )

4 The farmers _____ chickens. 그 농부들은 닭을 **기른다**.
( raise / feed )

5 They are neither bird nor _____. 그것들은 새도 **짐승**도 아니다.
( wild / beast )


**D** 우리말을 참고해서 알맞은 단어를 넣어 문장을 완성하세요.

1 The bear doesn't l_____ in this cave.
그 곰은 이 동굴에 **살지** 않는다.

2 The family lived in the w_____.
그 가족은 **야생**에서 살았다.

3 The fish are easy p_____ for birds.
물고기들은 새들의 쉬운 **먹이**다.

4 Lions are the king in the animal k_____.
사자는 동물의 **왕국**에서 왕이다.

5 We have to protect endangered s_____.
우리는 멸종 위기 **종**을 보호해야 한다.

# Plants 식물

| 01 | **water** | [wɔ́:tər] 물을 주다 |
|---|---|---|
| | water the garden  정원에 물을 주다 | |

| 02 | **stem** | [stem] 줄기 |
|---|---|---|
| | a thick stem  굵은 줄기 | |

| 03 | **root** | [ru(:)t] 뿌리 |
|---|---|---|
| | by the roots  뿌리째 | |

| 04 | **bloom** | [blu:m] 피다 |
|---|---|---|
| | bloom in spring  봄에 피다 | |

| 05 | **grow** | [grou] 자라다 |
|---|---|---|
| | grow tall  크게 자라다 | |

| 06 | **dense** | [dens] 빽빽한 |
|---|---|---|
| | dense forests  빽빽한 숲 | |

| 07 | **herb** | [ə:rb / hə:rb] 허브 |
|---|---|---|
| | learn about herbs  허브에 대해 배우다 | |

| 08 | **native** | [néitiv] 토종의, 태어난 |
|---|---|---|
| | native plants  토종 식물들 | |

| 09 | **thorn** | [θɔ:rn] 가시 |
|---|---|---|
| | without a thorn  가시 없는 | |

| 10 | **vary** | [vɛ́(:)əri] 다르다 |
|---|---|---|
| | vary in size  크기가 다르다 | |

✎ 영어 단어를 완성하세요.

1  water 물을 주다
   → ☐ater    w ☐ t ☐ r    ☐☐

2  stem 줄기
   → s ☐ em    ☐te    ☐☐

3  root 뿌리
   → r ☐ ot    ☐oo    ☐☐

4  bloom 피다
   → bloo ☐    ☐lo ☐ m    ☐☐

5  grow 자라다
   → g ☐ ow    ☐ro    ☐☐

6  dense 빽빽한
   → ☐ense    d ☐ ns ☐    ☐☐

7  herb 허브
   → he ☐ b    ☐er    ☐☐

8  native 토종의, 태어난
   → ☐ative    n ☐ tiv ☐    ☐☐

9  thorn 가시
   → t ☐ orn    ☐h ☐ rn    ☐☐

10 vary 다르다
   → v ☐ ry    ☐a ☐ y    ☐☐

# Practice

**A** 단어의 알맞은 뜻을 선으로 연결한 후, 빈칸에 단어를 직접 써보세요.

| 1 | thorn | • | | • | 자라다 | → | |
| 2 | herb | • | | • | 빽빽한 | → | |
| 3 | dense | • | | • | 허브 | → | |
| 4 | grow | • | | • | 가시 | → | |
| 5 | vary | • | | • | 다르다 | → | |

**B** 우리말과 일치하도록 빈칸에 알맞은 단어를 보기 에서 찾아 쓰세요.

| 보기 | water | stem | root | bloom | native |
|---|---|---|---|---|---|

1  토종 식물들          →  _____ plants

2  굵은 줄기            →  a thick _____

3  뿌리째              →  by the _____s

4  정원에 물을 주다      →  _____ the garden

5  봄에 피다            →  _____ in spring

**C** 우리말을 참고해서 빈칸에 알맞은 단어를 골라 문장을 완성하세요.

1 You can learn about _____. 너는 **허브**에 대해 배울 수 있다.
( herbs / stems )

2 Did you _____ the garden? 너는 정원에 **물을 줬니**?
( water / grow )

3 No rose without a _____. **가시** 없는 장미는 없다.
( thorn / root )

4 She pulled the plant up by the _____. 그녀는 그 식물을 **뿌리**째 뽑았다.
( herbs / roots )

5 A lot of flowers _____ in spring. 많은 꽃들이 봄에 **핀다**.
( vary / bloom )

**D** 우리말을 참고해서 알맞은 단어를 넣어 문장을 완성하세요.

1 Sunflowers g_____ tall quickly. 해바라기는 빨리 크게 **자란다**.

2 This is the n_____ plant of Korea. 이것은 한국 **토종** 식물이다.

3 Flowers v_____ in size and color. 꽃들은 크기와 색이 **다르다**.

4 She went through the d_____ forests. 그녀는 그 **빽빽한** 숲을 뚫고 갔다.

5 A cactus has a thick s_____. 선인장은 굵은 **줄기**가 있다.

# Insects 곤충

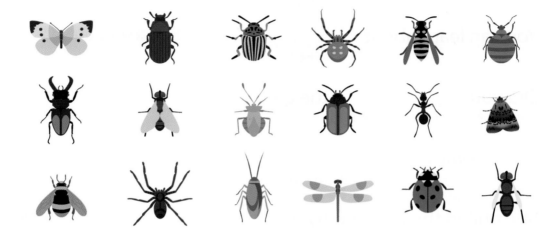

**01 insect** [ínsekt] 곤충

collect insects 곤충을 채집하다

**02 lay** [lei] 낳다

lay an egg 알을 낳다

**03 helpful** [hélpfəl] 이로운

helpful insects 이로운 곤충들

**04 harmful** [háːrmfəl] 해로운

be very harmful 매우 해롭다

**05 spray** [sprei] 뿌리다

spray pesticides 살충제를 뿌리다

**06 attack** [ətǽk] 공격하다

attack an enemy 적을 공격하다

**07 caterpillar** [kǽtərpilər] 애벌레

a green caterpillar 초록 애벌레

**08 hatch** [hætʃ] 부화하다

be about to hatch 막 부화하려 하다

**09 poison** [pɔ́izən] 독

a deadly poison 치명적인 독

**10 pest** [pest] 해충

diseases and pests 병해충

✎ 영어 단어를 완성하세요.

**1** insect 곤충

→ ins☐ct ☐n☐ect ☐☐

**2** lay 낳다

→ l☐y ☐a☐ ☐☐

**3** helpful 이로운

→ h☐lpful ☐el☐ful ☐☐

**4** harmful 해로운

→ har☐ful ☐arm☐ul ☐☐

**5** spray 뿌리다

→ ☐pray s☐r☐y ☐☐

**6** attack 공격하다

→ a☐tack ☐tt☐ck ☐☐

**7** caterpillar 애벌레

→ ca☐erpillar ☐ater☐illar ☐☐

**8** hatch 부화하다

→ h☐tch ☐a☐ch ☐☐

**9** poison 독

→ po☐son p☐is☐n ☐☐

**10** pest 해충

→ p☐st ☐es☐ ☐☐

# ✎ Practice

**A** 단어의 알맞은 뜻을 선으로 연결한 후, 빈칸에 단어를 직접 써보세요.

| 1 | pest | • | • | 곤충 | → | |
| 2 | helpful | • | • | 해충 | → | |
| 3 | poison | • | • | 낳다 | → | |
| 4 | insect | • | • | 이로운 | → | |
| 5 | lay | • | • | 독 | → | |

**B** 우리말과 일치하도록 빈칸에 알맞은 단어를 보기 에서 찾아 쓰세요.

| 보기 | spray | attack | caterpillar | hatch | harmful |

1 매우 해롭다 → be very _____

2 살충제를 뿌리다 → _____ pesticides

3 적을 공격하다 → _____ an enemy

4 초록 애벌레 → a green _____

5 막 부화하려 하다 → be about to _____

**C** 우리말을 참고해서 빈칸에 알맞은 단어를 골라 문장을 완성하세요.

1 He goes there to collect _____. 그는 **곤충**을 채집하러 거기에 간다.
( insects / pests )

2 Ten bees are about to _____. 벌 10마리가 막 **부화하려** 한다.
( spray / hatch )

3 Some mosquitoes are very _____. 어떤 모기들은 매우 **해롭**다.
( helpful / harmful )

4 Most insects _____ an egg. 대부분의 곤충들은 알을 **낳는다**.
( lay / hatch )

5 They worry about diseases and _____. 그들은 병**해충**에 대해 걱정한다.
( pests / poisons )

**D** 우리말을 참고해서 알맞은 단어를 넣어 문장을 완성하세요.

1 Some insects have a deadly p_____.
일부 곤충들은 치명적인 **독**이 있다.

2 They plan to a_____ the enemy.
그들은 그 적을 **공격할** 계획이다.

3 I saw a green c_____ on a leaf.
나는 잎 위에 있는 초록 **애벌레**를 봤다.

4 Spiders are very h_____ insects.
거미는 매우 **이로운** 곤충이다.

5 They s_____ pesticides to kill the pests.
그들은 그 해충들을 죽이기 위해 살충제를 **뿌린다**.

# Weather 날씨

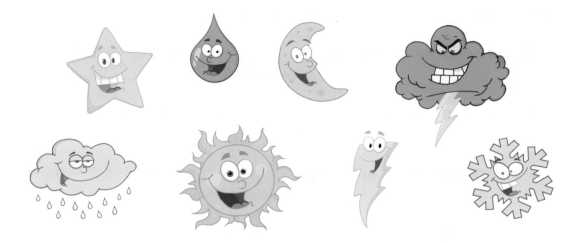

| 01 **warm** | [wɔːrm] 따뜻한 |
|---|---|
| warm in winter 겨울에 따뜻한 | |

| 02 **clear** | [kliər] 맑은 |
|---|---|
| on clear days 맑은 날에 | |

| 03 **cloudy** | [kláudi] 흐린 |
|---|---|
| be a little cloudy 약간 흐리다 | |

| 04 **cool** | [kuːl] 시원한 |
|---|---|
| cool in autumn 가을에 시원한 | |

| 05 **weather** | [wéðər] 날씨 |
|---|---|
| predict the weather 날씨를 예측하다 | |

| 06 **sunshine** | [sʌ́nʃàin] 햇빛, 햇살 |
|---|---|
| the spring sunshine 봄 햇살 | |

| 07 **lightning** | [láitniŋ] 번개 |
|---|---|
| like lightning 번개처럼 | |

| 08 **shower** | [ʃáuər] 소나기 |
|---|---|
| a sudden shower 갑작스런 소나기 | |

| 09 **forecast** | [fɔ́ːrkæ̀st] 예보 |
|---|---|
| a weather forecast 일기 예보 | |

| 10 **thunder** | [θʌ́ndər] 천둥 |
|---|---|
| hear the thunder 천둥소리를 듣다 | |

✎ 영어 단어를 완성하세요.

1  warm 따뜻한
→  w ☐ rm        ☐ ar ☐        ☐ ☐

2  clear 맑은
→  cl ☐ ar        ☐ lea ☐        ☐ ☐

3  cloudy 흐린
→  ☐ loudy        cl ☐ ud ☐        ☐ ☐

4  cool 시원한
→  c ☐ ol        ☐ oo ☐        ☐ ☐

5  weather 날씨
→  we ☐ ther        ☐ ea ☐ her        ☐ ☐

6  sunshine 햇빛, 햇살
→  suns ☐ ine        ☐ un ☐ hine        ☐ ☐

7  lightning 번개
→  ligh ☐ ning        ☐ ight ☐ ing        ☐ ☐

8  shower 소나기
→  sh ☐ wer        ☐ ho ☐ er        ☐ ☐

9  forecast 예보
→  fore ☐ ast        f ☐ rec ☐ st        ☐ ☐

10  thunder 천둥
→  ☐ hunder        th ☐ nd ☐ r        ☐ ☐

# Practice

**A** 단어의 알맞은 뜻을 선으로 연결한 후, 빈칸에 단어를 직접 써보세요.

| | | | |
|---|---|---|---|
| 1 | weather • | • 따뜻한 | → |
| 2 | sunshine • | • 맑은 | → |
| 3 | shower • | • 날씨 | → |
| 4 | clear • | • 햇빛, 햇살 | → |
| 5 | warm • | • 소나기 | → |

**B** 우리말과 일치하도록 빈칸에 알맞은 단어를 보기 에서 찾아 쓰세요.

보기   forecast   cool   lightning   thunder   cloudy

1  일기 예보   →   a weather _____

2  천둥소리를 듣다   →   hear the _____

3  약간 흐리다   →   be a little _____

4  가을에 시원한   →   _____ in autumn

5  번개처럼   →   like _____

**C** 우리말을 참고해서 빈칸에 알맞은 단어를 골라 문장을 완성하세요.

1  It keeps you _____ in winter.  그것은 겨울에 너를 **따뜻하게** 해준다.
( warm / cloudy )

2  Busan is _____ in autumn.  부산은 가을에 **시원하다**.
( cool / sunshine )

3  They move like _____.  그들은 **번개**처럼 움직인다.
( lightning / cloudy )

4  I didn't hear the _____.  나는 **천둥**소리를 듣지 못했다.
( lightning / thunder )

5  People try to predict the _____.  사람들은 **날씨**를 예측하려고 한다.
( forecast / weather )

**D** 우리말을 참고해서 알맞은 단어를 넣어 문장을 완성하세요.

1  According to the weather  f _____ , it is sunny today.
그 일기 **예보**에 의하면, 오늘은 맑다.

2  We enjoy the spring  s _____ .
우리는 봄 **햇살**을 즐긴다.

3  It is a little  c _____ here in Seoul.
여기 서울은 약간 **흐리**다.

4  On  c _____ days, I can see the Milky Way.
**맑은** 날에, 나는 은하수를 볼 수 있다.

5  The rainbow appeared after a sudden  s _____ .
갑작스런 **소나기** 뒤로 그 무지개가 나타났다.

# Traffic 교통

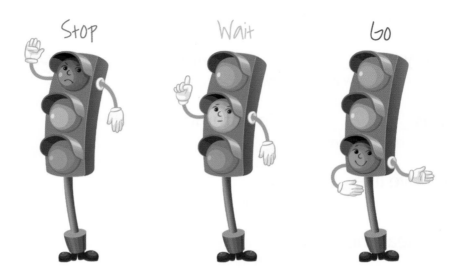

Stop    Wait    Go

**01 traffic** [trǽfik]
교통

a traffic sign 교통 표지판

**02 way** [wei]
길

find out the way 길을 찾다

**03 street** [striːt]
거리

on the street 거리에

**04 speed** [spiːd]
속도

at full speed 전속력으로

**05 pedestrian** [pədéstriən]
보행자

a careless pedestrian 부주의한 보행자

**06 signal** [sígnəl]
신호

a stop signal 정지 신호

**07 bumper** [bʌ́mpər]
범퍼

bumper to bumper 차가 꽉 찬(범퍼가 맞닿은)

**08 crosswalk** [krɔ́(ː)swɔ̀ːk]
횡단보도

cross at the crosswalk 횡단보도로 건너다

**09 parking** [páːrkiŋ]
주차

a parking lot 주차장

**10 tow** [tou]
견인

a tow truck 견인차

✎ 영어 단어를 완성하세요.

**1** traffic 교통

→ tr [ ] ffic    [ ] ra [ ] fic    [ ] [ ]

**2** way 길

→ w [ ] y    [ ] a [ ]    [ ] [ ]

**3** street 거리

→ [ ] treet    s [ ] ree [ ]    [ ] [ ]

**4** speed 속도

→ s [ ] eed    [ ] pee [ ]    [ ] [ ]

**5** pedestrian 보행자

→ pe [ ] estrian    [ ] edes [ ] rian    [ ] [ ]

**6** signal 신호

→ si [ ] nal    [ ] ig [ ] al    [ ] [ ]

**7** bumper 범퍼

→ bu [ ] per    [ ] um [ ] er    [ ] [ ]

**8** crosswalk 횡단보도

→ cro [ ] swalk    [ ] ross [ ] alk    [ ] [ ]

**9** parking 주차

→ parki [ ] g    [ ] ar [ ] ing    [ ] [ ]

**10** tow 견인

→ t [ ] w    [ ] o [ ]    [ ] [ ]

# Practice

**A** 단어의 알맞은 뜻을 선으로 연결한 후, 빈칸에 단어를 직접 써보세요.

1 signal • • 보행자 →
2 pedestrian • • 신호 →
3 traffic • • 범퍼 →
4 crosswalk • • 교통 →
5 bumper • • 횡단보도 →

**B** 우리말과 일치하도록 빈칸에 알맞은 단어를 보기 에서 찾아 쓰세요.

| 보기 | street | speed | way | parking | tow |
|------|--------|-------|-----|---------|-----|

1 거리에 → on the _____

2 전속력으로 → at full _____

3 주차장 → a _____ lot

4 견인차 → a _____ truck

5 길을 찾다 → find out the _____

**C**  우리말을 참고해서 빈칸에 알맞은 단어를 골라 문장을 완성하세요.

1   Jack looked at the _____ sign.  Jack은 그 **교통** 표지판을 보았다.
( bumper / traffic )

2   He drove his car at full _____.  그는 **전속력**으로 차를 몰았다.
( speed / street )

3   Let's cross at the _____.  **횡단보도**로 건너자.
( pedestrian / crosswalk )

4   A red light is a stop _____.  빨간 불빛이 정지 **신호**다.
( way / signal )

5   The building has a _____ lot.  그 건물은 **주차**장이 있다.
( tow / parking )


**D**  우리말을 참고해서 알맞은 단어를 넣어 문장을 완성하세요.

1   She called a  t_____  truck at night.
그녀는 밤에 **견인**차를 불렀다.

2   There are many cars on the  s_____.
그 **거리**에 자동차들이 많다.

3   We found out the  w_____ to get there.
우리는 거기에 가는 **길**을 찾았다.

4   The traffic is  b_____ to bumper on the road.
그 도로에 차들이 꽉 차(**범퍼**가 맞닿아) 있다.

5   A careless  p_____ causes traffic jams.
부주의한 **보행자**는 교통 체증을 야기한다.

**A** 다음 영어 단어의 우리말 뜻을 쓰세요.

1  lay          →  _____
2  species      →  _____
3  spray        →  _____
4  root         →  _____
5  caterpillar  →  _____
6  grow         →  _____
7  warm         →  _____
8  pest         →  _____
9  clear        →  _____
10 lightning    →  _____
11 way          →  _____
12 shower       →  _____
13 herb         →  _____
14 thunder      →  _____

**B** 다음 우리말을 보고 영어표현을 완성하세요.

1  r _____ chickens
   닭을 기르다

2  the spring s _____
   봄 햇살

3  l _____ in a cave
   동굴에서 살다

4  a weather f _____
   일기 예보

5  a thick s _____
   굵은 줄기

6  cross at the c _____
   횡단보도로 건너다

7  v _____ in size
   크기가 다르다

8  a t _____ truck
   견인차

9  be very h _____
   매우 해롭다

10 a p _____ lot
   주차장

11 be a little c _____
   약간 흐리다

12 in the w _____
   야생에서

13 the animal k _____
   동물의 왕국

14 neither bird nor b _____
   새도 짐승도 아닌

**C** 우리말과 같도록 괄호 안에서 알맞은 단어에 동그라미 하세요.

1  This is the ( native / domestic ) plant of Korea. 이것은 한국 **토종** 식물이다.

2  No rose without a ( thorn / stem ). **가시** 없는 장미는 없다.

3  He goes there to collect ( insects / animals ). 그는 **곤충**을 채집하러 거기에 간다.

4  They plan to ( spray / attack ) the enemy. 그들은 그 적을 **공격할** 계획이다.

5  Ten bees are about to ( hatch / grow ). 벌 10마리가 막 **부화하려** 한다.

6  Busan is ( cloudy / cool ) in autumn. 부산은 가을에 **시원하**다.

7  Jack looked at the ( traffic / wild ) sign. Jack은 그 **교통** 표지판을 보았다.

8  A red light is a stop ( speed / signal ). 빨간 불빛이 정지 **신호**다.

**D** 우리말과 같도록 다음 영어 문장을 완성하세요.

1  The fish are easy p_____ for birds. 물고기들은 새들의 쉬운 **먹이**다.

2  What do you f_____ the dog? 너는 그 개에게 무엇을 **먹이로 주니**?

3  Did you w_____ the garden? 너는 정원에 **물을 줬니**?

4  A lot of flowers b_____ in spring. 많은 꽃들이 봄에 **핀다**.

5  She went through the d_____ forests. 그녀는 그 **빽빽한** 숲을 뚫고 갔다.

6  Some insects have a deadly p_____. 일부 곤충들은 치명적인 **독**이 있다.

7  There are many cars on the s_____. 그 **거리**에 자동차들이 많다.

8  He drove his car at full s_____. 그는 **전속력**으로 차를 몰았다.

# Vehicles 탈것

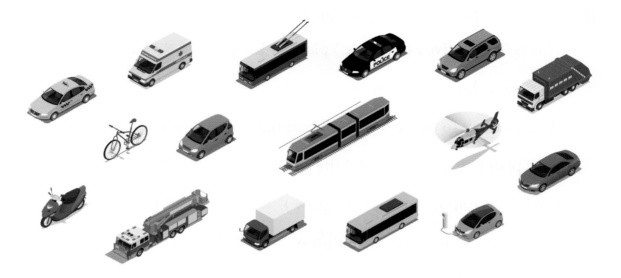

| 01 | **subway** [sʌ́bwèi] 지하철 |
|---|---|
| | by subway 지하철로 |

| 02 | **driver** [dráivər] 운전사 |
|---|---|
| | a taxi driver 택시 운전사 |

| 03 | **transfer** [trǽnsfər] 갈아타다 |
|---|---|
| | transfer to a train 기차로 갈아타다 |

| 04 | **fare** [fɛər] 요금 |
|---|---|
| | a bus fare 버스 요금 |

| 05 | **ticket** [tíkit] 티켓, 표 |
|---|---|
| | buy a ticket 티켓을 사다 |

| 06 | **broken** [bróukən] 고장 난 |
|---|---|
| | a broken elevator 고장 난 엘리베이터 |

| 07 | **underground** [ʌ̀ndərgráund] 지하의 |
|---|---|
| | an underground parking lot 지하 주차장 |

| 08 | **highway** [háiwèi] 고속도로 |
|---|---|
| | on a highway 고속도로에서 |

| 09 | **passenger** [pǽsəndʒər] 승객 |
|---|---|
| | all passengers 모든 승객들 |

| 10 | **area** [ɛ́əriə] 지역 |
|---|---|
| | go through this area 이 지역을 통과하다 |

✎ 영어 단어를 완성하세요.

1   subway  지하철

→   su ☐ way     ☐ ub ☐ ay

2   driver  운전사

→   dr ☐ ver     ☐ ri ☐ er

3   transfer  갈아타다

→   tra ☐ sfer     ☐ rans ☐ er

4   fare  요금

→   f ☐ re     ☐ a ☐ e

5   ticket  티켓, 표

→   ☐ icket     t ☐ ck ☐ t

6   broken  고장 난

→   br ☐ ken     ☐ ro ☐ en

7   underground  지하의

→   under ☐ round     und ☐ rgr ☐ und

8   highway  고속도로

→   hig ☐ way     ☐ igh ☐ ay

9   passenger  승객

→   passe ☐ ger     p ☐ ss ☐ nger

10   area  지역

→   a ☐ ea     ☐ r ☐ a

# ✎ Practice

**A**  단어의 알맞은 뜻을 선으로 연결한 후, 빈칸에 단어를 직접 써보세요.

| | | |
|---|---|---|
| 1 | passenger • | • 지하의 → _____ |
| 2 | underground • | • 승객 → _____ |
| 3 | transfer • | • 운전사 → _____ |
| 4 | area • | • 갈아타다 → _____ |
| 5 | driver • | • 지역 → _____ |

**B**  우리말과 일치하도록 빈칸에 알맞은 단어를 보기 에서 찾아 쓰세요.

보기    fare    broken    subway    highway    ticket

1  지하철로 → by _____

2  버스 요금 → a bus _____

3  티켓을 사다 → buy a _____

4  고장 난 엘리베이터 → a _____ elevator

5  고속도로에서 → on a _____

**C** 우리말을 참고해서 빈칸에 알맞은 단어를 골라 문장을 완성하세요.

1 He went to the museum by _____. 그는 **지하철**로 박물관에 갔다.
( subway / highway )

2 All _____ on the bus are students. 그 버스의 모든 **승객들**은 학생이다.
( drivers / passengers )

3 Is your uncle a taxi _____? 네 삼촌은 택시 **운전사**니?
( driver / fare )

4 I have to _____ to a train. 나는 기차로 **갈아타야** 한다.
( transfer / broken )

5 You must buy a _____ for Busan. 너는 부산행 **티켓**을 사야 한다.
( fare / ticket )


**D** 우리말을 참고해서 알맞은 단어를 넣어 문장을 완성하세요.

1 They fixed the b_____ elevator.
그들은 **고장 난** 엘리베이터를 고쳤다.

2 Paul parked in an u_____ parking lot.
Paul은 **지하** 주차장에 주차했다.

3 There was an accident on a h_____.
**고속도로**에서 사고가 있었다.

4 Bus f_____s will go up next month.
버스 **요금**이 다음달 오를 것이다.

5 The bus goes through this a_____.
그 버스는 이 **지역**을 통과한다.

# Technology 기술

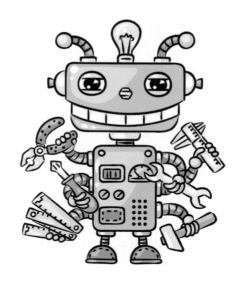

**01 invent** [invént]
발명하다
invent a telephone 전화를 발명하다

**02 technology** [teknáɫədʒi]
(과학) 기술
high technology 첨단 기술

**03 machine** [məʃíːn]
기계
a washing machine 세탁기(세탁 기계)

**04 energy** [énərdʒi]
에너지
wind energy 풍력 에너지

**05 creative** [krieitiv]
창의적인
creative thinking 창의적 사고

**06 charge** [tʃɑːrdʒ]
충전하다
charge a smartphone 스마트폰을 충전하다

**07 digital** [dídʒitəl]
디지털의
a digital camera 디지털 카메라

**08 develop** [divéləp]
개발하다
develop new products 신제품을 개발하다

**09 switch** [switʃ]
스위치
a power switch 전원 스위치

**10 basic** [béisik]
기초의
basic science 기초 과학

영어 단어를 완성하세요.

**1**  invent 발명하다

→ in ◻ ent   |   i ◻ ven ◻   |   ◻

**2**  technology (과학) 기술

→ tec ◻ nology   |   ◻ ech ◻ ology   |   ◻

**3**  machine 기계

→ m ◻ chine   |   ◻ a ◻ hine   |   ◻

**4**  energy 에너지

→ ◻ nergy   |   en ◻ r ◻ y   |   ◻

**5**  creative 창의적인

→ ◻ reative   |   cre ◻ tiv ◻   |   ◻

**6**  charge 충전하다

→ ch ◻ rge   |   ◻ har ◻ e   |   ◻

**7**  digital 디지털의

→ di ◻ ital   |   ◻ igi ◻ al   |   ◻

**8**  develop 개발하다

→ de ◻ elop   |   ◻ evel ◻ p   |   ◻

**9**  switch 스위치

→ sw ◻ tch   |   s ◻ itc ◻   |   ◻

**10**  basic 기초의

→ ◻ asic   |   b ◻ s ◻ c   |   ◻

# Practice

## A 단어의 알맞은 뜻을 선으로 연결한 후, 빈칸에 단어를 직접 써보세요.

1 digital • • 충전하다 →
2 charge • • 발명하다 →
3 technology • • 디지털의 →
4 machine • • (과학) 기술 →
5 invent • • 기계 →

## B 우리말과 일치하도록 빈칸에 알맞은 단어를 보기 에서 찾아 쓰세요.

| 보기 | energy | develop | creative | switch | basic |

1 풍력 에너지 → wind _____

2 창의적 사고 → _____ thinking

3 기초 과학 → _____ science

4 신제품을 개발하다 → _____ new products

5 전원 스위치 → a power _____

**C** 우리말을 참고해서 빈칸에 알맞은 단어를 골라 문장을 완성하세요.

1 Graham Bell _____ a telephone. Graham Bell은 전화를 **발명했다**.
( invented / charged )

2 High _____ will change our lives. 첨단 **기술**이 우리의 삶을 변화시킬 것이다.
( digital / technology )

3 He can fix a washing _____. 그는 세탁기(세탁 **기계**)를 고칠 수 있다.
( energy / machine )

4 He has to _____ his smartphone. 그는 그의 스마트폰을 **충전해야** 한다.
( charge / switch )

5 I bought a _____ camera. 나는 **디지털** 카메라를 샀다.
( basic / digital )

**D** 우리말을 참고해서 알맞은 단어를 넣어 문장을 완성하세요.

1 The city will use wind e_____.
그 도시는 풍력 **에너지**를 사용할 것이다.

2 The company needs people with c_____ thinking.
그 회사는 **창의적** 사고를 하는 사람들이 필요하다.

3 Scientists d_____ new products every year.
과학자들은 매년 신제품을 **개발한다**.

4 He turned off the power s_____.
그는 그 전원 **스위치**를 껐다.

5 The study on b_____ science is important.
**기초** 과학에 대한 연구가 중요하다.

# Earth & Universe 지구와 우주

| | |
|---|---|
| **01** **earth** [ə:rθ] 지구 <br> on the earth  지구에 | **02** **forest** [fɔ́(:)rist] 숲 <br> in the forest  숲에 |
| **03** **ocean** [óuʃən] 바다, 대양 <br> an ocean view  바다 경치 | **04** **Pacific** [pəsífik] 태평양 <br> in the Western Pacific  서태평양에 |
| **05** **valley** [vǽli] 계곡 <br> go to valleys  계곡으로 가다 | **06** **desert** [dézərt] 사막 <br> survive in a desert  사막에서 살아남다 |
| **07** **space** [speis] 우주 <br> travel in space  우주를 여행하다 | **08** **spaceship** [spéisʃip] 우주선 <br> send a spaceship to Mars  우주선을 화성에 보내다 |
| **09** **astronaut** [ǽstrənɔ̀:t] 우주비행사 <br> become an astronaut  우주비행사가 되다 | **10** **planet** [plǽnit] 행성 <br> the smallest planet  가장 작은 행성 |

✏️ 영어 단어를 완성하세요.

**1** earth 지구

→ e ☐ rth ☐ ar ☐ h ☐ ☐

**2** forest 숲

→ fores ☐ f ☐ r ☐ st ☐ ☐

**3** ocean 바다, 대양

→ oc ☐ an ☐ ce ☐ n ☐ ☐

**4** Pacific 태평양

→ Pa ☐ ific Paci ☐ i ☐ ☐ ☐

**5** valley 계곡

→ v ☐ lley ☐ all ☐ y ☐ ☐

**6** desert 사막

→ d ☐ sert ☐ es ☐ rt ☐ ☐

**7** space 우주

→ s ☐ ace ☐ p ☐ ce ☐ ☐

**8** spaceship 우주선

→ sp ☐ ceship ☐ pace ☐ hip ☐ ☐

**9** astronaut 우주비행사

→ astr ☐ naut ☐ stron ☐ ut ☐ ☐

**10** planet 행성

→ pl ☐ net ☐ lane ☐ ☐ ☐

# ✎ Practice

**A** 단어의 알맞은 뜻을 선으로 연결한 후, 빈칸에 단어를 직접 써보세요.

1  valley  •                •  우주선     →  [          ]

2  astronaut  •             •  계곡        →  [          ]

3  spaceship  •             •  태평양      →  [          ]

4  planet  •                •  우주비행사   →  [          ]

5  Pacific  •               •  행성        →  [          ]


**B** 우리말과 일치하도록 빈칸에 알맞은 단어를 보기 에서 찾아 쓰세요.

| 보기 | desert | forest | space | earth | ocean |

1  우주를 여행하다        →  travel in _____

2  지구에                →  on the _____

3  숲에                  →  in the _____

4  바다 경치             →  an _____ view

5  사막에서 살아남다      →  survive in a _____

**C** 우리말을 참고해서 빈칸에 알맞은 단어를 골라 문장을 완성하세요.

1 I want to travel in _____ someday. 나는 언젠가 **우주**를 여행하고 싶다.
   ( space / spaceship )

2 His dream is to become an _____. 그의 꿈은 **우주비행사**가 되는 것이다.
   ( planet / astronaut )

3 People go to _____ to flee the heat. 사람들은 더위를 피하기 위해 **계곡**으로 간다.
   ( valleys / oceans )

4 It lives in the Western _____. 그것은 서**태평양**에 산다.
   ( Pacific / Forest )

5 There are countless insects on the _____. **지구**에는 수많은 곤충들이 살고 있다.
   ( earth / desert )

**D** 우리말을 참고해서 알맞은 단어를 넣어 문장을 완성하세요.

1 There are many trees in the f_____.
   숲에 나무들이 많다.

2 They have a room with an o_____ view.
   그들은 **바다** 경치가 보이는 방이 있다.

3 Mercury is the smallest p_____.
   수성은 가장 작은 **행성**이다.

4 He can survive in a d_____.
   그는 **사막**에서 살아남을 수 있다.

5 They hope to send a s_____ to Mars.
   그들은 **우주선**을 화성에 보내기를 희망한다.

# Restaurants 식당

| 01 | **restaurant** | [réstərənt] 식당 |
|---|---|---|
| | a nice restaurant  멋진 식당 | |

| 02 | **menu** | [ménju:] 메뉴 |
|---|---|---|
| | on the menu  메뉴에서 | |

| 03 | **order** | [ɔ́:rdər] 주문하다 |
|---|---|---|
| | order chicken  치킨을 주문하다 | |

| 04 | **make** | [meik] 만들다 |
|---|---|---|
| | make pizza for us  우리를 위해 피자를 만들다 | |

| 05 | **reserve** | [rizə́:rv] 예약하다 |
|---|---|---|
| | reserve a table  자리를 예약하다 | |

| 06 | **waiter** | [wéitər] 종업원 |
|---|---|---|
| | work as a waiter  종업원으로 일하다 | |

| 07 | **chef** | [ʃef] 요리사 |
|---|---|---|
| | a head chef  수석 요리사 | |

| 08 | **medium** | [mí:diəm] 중간의 |
|---|---|---|
| | a medium heat  중간 온도 | |

| 09 | **tip** | [tip] 팁을 주다 |
|---|---|---|
| | tip waiters  종업원들에게 팁을 주다 | |

| 10 | **well-done** | [wel-dʌn] 잘 익힌 |
|---|---|---|
| | a steak well-done  잘 익힌 스테이크 | |

✎ 영어 단어를 완성하세요.

1  **restaurant** 식당

→  res ⬚ aurant      rest ⬚ ur ⬚ nt      ⬚ | ⬚

2  **menu** 메뉴

→  m ⬚ nu      ⬚ e ⬚ u      ⬚ | ⬚

3  **order** 주문하다

→  o ⬚ der      ⬚ r ⬚ er      ⬚ | ⬚

4  **make** 만들다

→  ⬚ ake      m ⬚ k ⬚      ⬚ | ⬚

5  **reserve** 예약하다

→  re ⬚ erve      ⬚ eser ⬚ e      ⬚ | ⬚

6  **waiter** 종업원

→  wa ⬚ ter      ⬚ ai ⬚ er      ⬚ | ⬚

7  **chef** 요리사

→  c ⬚ ef      ⬚ h ⬚ f      ⬚ | ⬚

8  **medium** 중간의

→  me ⬚ ium      ⬚ edi ⬚ m      ⬚ | ⬚

9  **tip** 팁을 주다

→  t ⬚ p      ⬚ i ⬚      ⬚ | ⬚

10  **well-done** 잘 익힌

→  w ⬚ ll-done      ⬚ ell- ⬚ one      ⬚ | ⬚

# Practice

**A** 단어의 알맞은 뜻을 선으로 연결한 후, 빈칸에 단어를 직접 써보세요.

1 well-done •  • 주문하다 →

2 order •  • 잘 익힌 →

3 menu •  • 만들다 →

4 make •  • 식당 →

5 restaurant •  • 메뉴 →

**B** 우리말과 일치하도록 빈칸에 알맞은 단어를 보기 에서 찾아 쓰세요.

| 보기 | reserve | waiter | chef | medium | tip |
|------|---------|--------|------|--------|-----|

1 자리를 예약하다 → _____ a table

2 수석 요리사 → a head _____

3 중간 온도 → a _____ heat

4 종업원들에게 팁을 주다 → _____ waiters

5 종업원으로 일하다 → work as a _____

**C** 우리말을 참고해서 빈칸에 알맞은 단어를 골라 문장을 완성하세요.

1 They _____ pizza for us. 그들은 우리를 위해 피자를 **만든다**.
　　( make / order )

2 Cook over a _____ heat. **중간** 온도 이상에서 요리해라.
　　( well-done / medium )

3 We went to a nice _____. 우리는 멋진 **식당**에 갔다.
　　( restaurant / chef )

4 You can find it on the _____. 너는 그 **메뉴**에서 그것을 찾을 수 있다.
　　( menu / waiter )

5 We sometimes _____ chicken. 우리는 때때로 치킨을 **주문한다**.
　　( tip / order )

**D** 우리말을 참고해서 알맞은 단어를 넣어 문장을 완성하세요.

1 I'd like to r_____ a table for three.
나는 세 명 자리를 **예약하고** 싶다.

2 He works as a w_____ at the restaurant.
그는 식당에서 **종업원**으로 일한다.

3 They are the head c_____s from France.
그들은 프랑스에서 온 수석 **요리사들**이다.

4 I prefer my steak w_____.
나는 **잘 익힌** 스테이크를 선호한다.

5 We don't have to t_____ waiters at restaurants.
우리는 식당에서 종업원들에게 **팁을 줄** 필요가 없다.

# Postal Service 우편서비스

**01 post office** [póust ɔ:fis] 우체국
at a post office 우체국에서

**02 envelope** [énvəlòup] 봉투
in an envelope 봉투 안에

**03 postcard** [poustka:rd] 엽서
get a postcard 엽서를 받다

**04 package** [pǽkidʒ] 소포
send a package 소포를 보내다

**05 form** [fɔ:rm] 서식, 양식
fill out this form 이 양식을 작성하다

**06 airmail** [ɛ́ərmèil] 항공 우편
by airmail 항공 우편으로

**07 zip code** [zip koud] 우편 번호
enter a zip code 우편 번호를 입력하다

**08 direct** [dirékt] 직접적인
direct mail 다이렉트(직접) 메일

**09 regular** [régjulər] 보통의
regular mail 보통 우편

**10 express** [ikspres] 속달의
express mail 속달 우편

✎ 영어 단어를 완성하세요.

**1** post office 우체국

→ post o ☐ fice | ☐ ost ☐ ffice | ☐ ☐

**2** envelope 봉투

→ e ☐ velope | env ☐ lo ☐ e | ☐ ☐

**3** postcard 엽서

→ pos ☐ card | ☐ ost ☐ ard | ☐ ☐

**4** package 소포

→ ☐ ackage | p ☐ ck ☐ ge | ☐ ☐

**5** form 서식, 양식

→ f ☐ rm | ☐ or ☐ | ☐ ☐

**6** airmail 항공 우편

→ air ☐ ail | ☐ irm ☐ il | ☐ ☐

**7** zip code 우편 번호

→ zip c ☐ de | ☐ ip ☐ ode | ☐ ☐

**8** direct 직접적인

→ ☐ irect | d ☐ r ☐ ct | ☐ ☐

**9** regular 보통의

→ re ☐ ular | r ☐ gul ☐ r | ☐ ☐

**10** express 속달의

→ ex ☐ ress | ☐ xpr ☐ ss | ☐ ☐

# Practice

**A** 단어의 알맞은 뜻을 선으로 연결한 후, 빈칸에 단어를 직접 써보세요.

| 1 | postcard | • | • | 우편 번호 | → | |
|---|----------|---|---|-----------|---|---|
| 2 | zip code | • | • | 우체국 | → | |
| 3 | package | • | • | 봉투 | → | |
| 4 | envelope | • | • | 엽서 | → | |
| 5 | post office | • | • | 소포 | → | |

**B** 우리말과 일치하도록 빈칸에 알맞은 단어를 보기 에서 찾아 쓰세요.

| 보기 | form | express | airmail | direct | regular |
|------|------|---------|---------|--------|---------|

1 다이렉트(직접) 메일 → _____ mail

2 보통 우편 → _____ mail

3 항공 우편으로 → by _____

4 이 양식을 작성하다 → fill out this _____

5 속달 우편 → _____ mail

**C** 우리말을 참고해서 빈칸에 알맞은 단어를 골라 문장을 완성하세요.

1  We buy stamps at a _____. 우리는 **우체국**에서 우표를 산다.
( post office / express )

2  She put the letter in an _____. 그녀는 그 편지를 **봉투** 안에 넣었다.
( envelope / form )

3  Send this package by _____. 이 소포를 **항공 우편**으로 보내라.
( airmail / regular )

4  I look forward to getting your _____. 나는 네 **엽서**를 받길 기대한다.
( postcard / package )

5  Can you enter your _____? 너는 네 **우편 번호**를 입력할 수 있니?
( zip code / direct )

**D** 우리말을 참고해서 알맞은 단어를 넣어 문장을 완성하세요.

1  I sent a  p _____ yesterday.
나는 **소포**를 어제 보냈다.

2  Please tell me how to fill out this  f _____.
이 **양식**을 작성하는 방법을 말해 주세요.

3  He got an  e _____ mail in the morning.
그는 아침에 **속달** 우편을 받았다.

4  I will send it by  r _____ mail.
나는 그것을 **보통** 우편으로 보낼 것이다.

5  The store sends  d _____ mail to customers.
그 상점은 다이렉트(**직접**) 메일을 고객에게 보낸다.

## A 다음 영어 단어의 우리말 뜻을 쓰세요.

1 fare → _____  2 menu → _____

3 broken → _____  4 postcard → _____

5 develop → _____  6 direct → _____

7 planet → _____  8 package → _____

9 well-done → _____  10 express → _____

11 post office → _____  12 underground → _____

13 zip code → _____  14 restaurant → _____

## B 다음 우리말을 보고 영어표현을 완성하세요.

1 b_____ science
기초 과학

2 buy a t_____
티켓을 사다

3 travel in s_____
우주를 여행하다

4 c_____ thinking
창의적 사고

5 send a s_____ to Mars
우주선을 화성에 보내다

6 r_____ a table
자리를 예약하다

7 an o_____ view
바다 경치

8 t_____ waiters
종업원들에게 팁을 주다

9 survive in a d_____
사막에서 살아남다

10 fill out this f_____
이 양식을 작성하다

11 by a_____
항공 우편으로

12 by s_____
지하철로

13 wind e_____
풍력 에너지

14 on a h_____
고속도로에서

**C** 우리말과 같도록 괄호 안에서 알맞은 단어에 동그라미 하세요.

1 The bus goes through this ( area / planet ). 그 버스는 이 **지역**을 통과한다.

2 Graham Bell ( charged / invented ) a telephone. Graham Bell은 전화를 **발명했다**.

3 There are many trees in the ( ocean / forest ). 숲에 나무들이 많다.

4 He works as a ( waiter / chef ) at the restaurant. 그는 식당에서 **종업원**으로 일한다.

5 We sometimes ( order / charge ) chicken. 우리는 때때로 치킨을 **주문한다**.

6 They ( tip / make ) pizza for us. 그들은 우리를 위해 피자를 **만든다**.

7 She put the letter in an ( envelope / package ). 그녀는 그 편지를 **봉투** 안에 넣었다.

8 I have to ( transfer / switch ) to a train. 나는 기차로 **갈아타야** 한다.

**D** 우리말과 같도록 다음 영어 문장을 완성하세요.

1 Is your uncle a taxi d_____ ? 네 삼촌은 택시 **운전사니**?

2 He can fix a washing m_____ . 그는 세탁기(세탁 **기계**)를 고칠 수 있다.

3 He has to c_____ his smartphone. 그는 그의 스마트폰을 **충전해야** 한다.

4 I bought a d_____ camera. 나는 **디지털** 카메라를 샀다.

5 He turned off the power s_____ . 그는 그 전원 **스위치**를 껐다.

6 There are countless insects on the e_____ . **지구**에는 수많은 곤충들이 살고 있다.

7 People go to v_____ s to flee the heat. 사람들은 더위를 피하기 위해 **계곡**으로 간다.

8 They are the head c_____ s from France. 그들은 프랑스에서 온 수석 **요리사들**이다.

# Security 보안, 안전

01 **fire** [fáiər] 불, 화재

set fire to cars  자동차들에 불을 지르다

02 **call** [kɔːl] 전화

get a call  전화를 받다

03 **help** [help] 도움

with his help  그의 도움으로

04 **thief** [θiːf] 도둑

catch a thief  도둑을 잡다

05 **steal** [stiːl] 훔치다

steal a car  차를 훔치다

06 **save** [seiv] 구하다

save the forest  숲을 구하다

07 **fire station** [fáiər stéiʃən] 소방서

at a fire station  소방서에서

08 **police office** [pəlíːs ɔ́:fis] 경찰서

the nearest police office  가장 가까운 경찰서

09 **firefighter** [fáiərfáitər] 소방관

become a firefighter  소방관이 되다

10 **policeman** [pəlíːsmən] 경찰관

a brave policeman  용감한 경찰관

✎ 영어 단어를 완성하세요.

**1** fire 불, 화재

→ f ☐ re   ☐ i ☐ e   ☐ ☐

**2** call 전화

→ c ☐ ll   ☐ al ☐   ☐ ☐

**3** help 도움

→ h ☐ lp   ☐ el ☐   ☐ ☐

**4** thief 도둑

→ t ☐ ief   ☐ hie ☐   ☐ ☐

**5** steal 훔치다

→ s ☐ eal   ☐ te ☐ l   ☐ ☐

**6** save 구하다

→ s ☐ ve   ☐ a ☐ e   ☐ ☐

**7** fire station 소방서

→ fire st ☐ tion   ☐ ire ☐ tation   ☐ ☐

**8** police office 경찰서

→ police ☐ ffice   ☐ olice o ☐ fice   ☐ ☐

**9** firefighter 소방관

→ fire ☐ ighter   fir ☐ fight ☐ r   ☐ ☐

**10** policeman 경찰관

→ polic ☐ man   ☐ olice ☐ an   ☐ ☐

# ✎ Practice

A  단어의 알맞은 뜻을 선으로 연결한 후, 빈칸에 단어를 직접 써보세요.

| | | | |
|---|---|---|---|
| 1 | fire station • | • 도둑 | → |
| 2 | police office • | • 훔치다 | → |
| 3 | thief • | • 소방서 | → |
| 4 | firefighter • | • 경찰서 | → |
| 5 | steal • | • 소방관 | → |

B  우리말과 일치하도록 빈칸에 알맞은 단어를 보기 에서 찾아 쓰세요.

보기    policeman    save    fire    call    help

1  용감한 경찰관        →    a brave _____

2  자동차들에 불을 지르다   →    set _____ to cars

3  숲을 구하다           →    _____ the forest

4  전화를 받다           →    get a _____

5  그의 도움으로         →    with his _____

**C** 우리말을 참고해서 빈칸에 알맞은 단어를 골라 문장을 완성하세요.

**1** The little girl _____ the forest. 그 어린 소녀가 숲을 **구했다**.
( saved / called )

**2** I volunteered at the _____. 나는 **소방서**에서 자원봉사를 했다.
( fire station / police office )

**3** This man is planning to _____ a car. 이 남자는 차를 **훔칠** 계획 중이다.
( save / steal )

**4** Where is the nearest _____? 가장 가까운 **경찰서**가 어디에 있니?
( police office / fire station )

**5** The kid set _____ to cars. 그 아이가 자동차들에 **불**을 질렀다.
( thief / fire )

**D** 우리말을 참고해서 알맞은 단어를 넣어 문장을 완성하세요.

**1** I got a c_____ to cry for help.
나는 도와달라는 **전화**를 받았다.

**2** We put out the fire with his h_____.
우리는 그의 **도움**으로 불을 껐다.

**3** Did he catch a t_____ yesterday?
그는 어제 **도둑**을 잡았니?

**4** The boy wants to become a f_____.
그 소년은 **소방관**이 되고 싶어 한다.

**5** A brave p_____ caught the robber.
한 용감한 **경찰관**이 그 강도를 잡았다.

# Museums 박물관

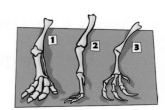

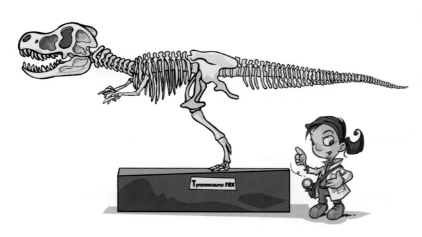

| 01 **museum** | [mjuːzíːəm] 박물관 |
|---|---|
| visit the museum 박물관을 방문하다 | |

| 02 **visitor** | [vízitər] 방문객 |
|---|---|
| many visitors 많은 방문객들 | |

| 03 **palace** | [pǽlis] 궁전 |
|---|---|
| an old palace 고궁(오래된 궁전) | |

| 04 **record** | [rékərd] 기록 |
|---|---|
| an amazing record 놀라운 기록 | |

| 05 **royal** | [rɔ́iəl] 왕(실)의 |
|---|---|
| royal blood 왕실의 피 | |

| 06 **guidebook** | [gáidbùk] 안내서 |
|---|---|
| a Korean guidebook 한국어 안내서 | |

| 07 **thing** | [θiŋ] 물건 |
|---|---|
| display the old things 옛 물건들을 전시하다 | |

| 08 **outstanding** | [àutstǽndiŋ] 뛰어난 |
|---|---|
| an outstanding exhibit 뛰어난 전시품 | |

| 09 **treasure** | [tréʒər] 보물 |
|---|---|
| a treasure map 보물 지도 | |

| 10 **exhibition** | [èksəbíʃən] 전시회 |
|---|---|
| a special exhibition 특별 전시회 | |

✏️ 영어 단어를 완성하세요.

**1**  museum 박물관

→  mus ☐ um          ☐ use ☐ m          ☐ | ☐

**2**  visitor 방문하다

→  visi ☐ or          ☐ isit ☐ r          ☐ | ☐

**3**  palace 궁전

→  ☐ alace          p ☐ l ☐ ce          ☐ | ☐

**4**  record 기록

→  ☐ ecord          r ☐ c ☐ rd          ☐ | ☐

**5**  royal 왕(실)의

→  r ☐ yal          ☐ o ☐ al          ☐ | ☐

**6**  guidebook 안내서

→  gu ☐ debook          ☐ ui ☐ ebook          ☐ | ☐

**7**  thing 물건

→  ☐ hing          t ☐ in ☐          ☐ | ☐

**8**  outstanding 뛰어난

→  out ☐ tanding          ☐ utstan ☐ ing          ☐ | ☐

**9**  treasure 보물

→  tre ☐ sure          ☐ rea ☐ ure          ☐ | ☐

**10**  exhibition 전시회

→  exhi ☐ ition          ex ☐ ibi ☐ ion          ☐ | ☐

# Practice

**A** 단어의 알맞은 뜻을 선으로 연결한 후, 빈칸에 단어를 직접 써보세요.

1  museum • — • 물건 →

2  thing • — • 박물관 →

3  treasure • — • 뛰어난 →

4  visitor • — • 보물 →

5  outstanding • — • 방문객 →

**B** 우리말과 일치하도록 빈칸에 알맞은 단어를 보기 에서 찾아 쓰세요.

| 보기 | record | royal | guidebook | exhibition | palace |
|------|--------|-------|-----------|------------|--------|

1  고궁(오래된 궁전)    →    an old _____

2  왕실의 피    →    _____ blood

3  한국어 안내서    →    a Korean _____

4  특별 전시회    →    a special _____

5  놀라운 기록    →    an amazing _____

**C** 우리말을 참고해서 빈칸에 알맞은 단어를 골라 문장을 완성하세요.

1 What an amazing _____ it is! 그것은 놀라운 **기록**이구나!
( thing / record )

2 _____ blood flows in our veins. 왕실의 피가 우리의 혈관에 흐른다.
( Royal / Palace )

3 This is the most _____ exhibit. 이것은 가장 **뛰어난** 전시품이다.
( outstanding / treasure )

4 They display the old _____. 그들은 옛 **물건들**을 전시한다.
( things / records )

5 When do they visit the _____? 그들은 **박물관**을 언제 방문하니?
( museum / palace )

**D** 우리말을 참고해서 알맞은 단어를 넣어 문장을 완성하세요.

1 There are many v_____s to the museum.
그 박물관에 오는 **방문객들**이 많다.

2 We can get Korean g_____s at the museum.
우리는 그 박물관에서 한국어 **안내서**를 받을 수 있다.

3 The scientist found a t_____ map.
그 과학자는 **보물** 지도를 발견했다.

4 We are interested in the special e_____.
우리는 그 특별 **전시회**에 관심이 있다.

5 The old p_____ will be a national museum.
그 고궁(오래된 **궁전**)은 국립박물관이 될 것이다.

# Health Care 의료서비스

| 01 **pain** | [pein] 고통 |
|---|---|
| feel much pain 많은 고통을 느끼다 | |

| 02 **sick** | [sik] 아픈, 병든 |
|---|---|
| get sick 병들다 | |

| 03 **clinic** | [klínik] 진료소 |
|---|---|
| a health clinic 건강 진료소 | |

| 04 **shot** | [ʃat] 주사 |
|---|---|
| get a flu shot 독감 주사를 맞다 | |

| 05 **hospital** | [háspitəl] 병원 |
|---|---|
| stay in the hospital 입원하다(병원에 머무르다) | |

| 06 **patient** | [péiʃənt] 환자 |
|---|---|
| take care of patients 환자들을 돌보다 | |

| 07 **checkup** | [tʃékλp] 건강검진 |
|---|---|
| a special checkup 특별한 건강검진 | |

| 08 **serious** | [sí(:)əriəs] 심각한 |
|---|---|
| a serious problem 심각한 문제 | |

| 09 **flu** | [flu:] 독감 |
|---|---|
| catch the flu 독감에 걸리다 | |

| 10 **symptom** | [símptəm] 증상 |
|---|---|
| a common symptom 흔한 증상 | |

영어 단어를 완성하세요.

1  pain 고통
→  p  in        ai

2  sick 아픈, 병든
→  s  ck        i  k

3  clinic 진료소
→  cli  ic      cl  n  c

4  shot 주사
→  s  ot        h  t

5  hospital 병원
→  hos  ital    ospi  al

6  patient 환자
→  atient       p  ti  nt

7  checkup 건강검진
→  ch  ckup     heck  p

8  serious 심각한
→  erious       s  ri  us

9  flu 독감
→  f  u         l

10  symptom 증상
→  ymptom       sy  pto

# Practice

**A** 단어의 알맞은 뜻을 선으로 연결한 후, 빈칸에 단어를 직접 써보세요.

1 clinic • • 아픈, 병든 →
2 pain • • 진료소 →
3 sick • • 고통 →
4 patient • • 환자 →
5 symptom • • 증상 →

**B** 우리말과 일치하도록 빈칸에 알맞은 단어를 보기 에서 찾아 쓰세요.

| 보기 | flu | shot | checkup | hospital | serious |
|------|-----|------|---------|----------|---------|

1 독감 주사를 맞다 → get a flu _____

2 특별한 건강검진 → a special _____

3 심각한 문제 → a _____ problem

4 독감에 걸리다 → catch the _____

5 입원하다(병원에 머무르다) → stay in the _____

**C** 우리말을 참고해서 빈칸에 알맞은 단어를 골라 문장을 완성하세요.

1  A doctor is taking care of _____. 한 의사가 **환자들**을 돌보고 있다.
   ( patients / hospitals )

2  It has gyms, health _____, and more. 그곳에는 체육관, 건강 **진료소** 등이 있다.
   ( clinics / symptoms )

3  You have to get a flu _____. 너는 독감 **주사**를 맞아야 한다.
   ( pain / shot )

4  Do you feel much _____? 너는 많은 **고통**을 느끼니?
   ( serious / pain )

5  You can get _____ easily. 너는 쉽게 **병들** 수 있다.
   ( sick / shot )


**D** 우리말을 참고해서 알맞은 단어를 넣어 문장을 완성하세요.

1  He has to stay in the  h _____.
   그는 입원해야(**병원**에 머물러야) 한다.

2  It is easy to catch the  f _____ these days.
   요즘은 **독감**에 걸리기 쉽다.

3  Sneezing is also a common  s _____.
   재채기도 또한 흔한 **증상**이다.

4  The government provides a special  c _____.
   정부에서 특별한 **건강검진**을 제공한다.

5  Child obesity is a  s _____ problem.
   아동비만은 **심각한** 문제다.

# Movies 영화

**01 theater** [θí(ː)ətər] 극장
go to the theater 극장에 가다

**02 movie** [múːvi] 영화
show a movie 영화를 상영하다

**03 action** [ǽkʃən] 액션
an action movie 액션 영화

**04 preview** [príːvjùː] 시사회
a press preview 기자 시사회

**05 horror** [hɔ́(ː)rər] 공포
a horror film 공포 영화

**06 fantasy** [fǽntəsi] 상상, 공상
in a fantasy world 상상 세계에서

**07 mystery** [místəri] 미스터리
be filled with mystery 미스터리로 가득 차다

**08 trailer** [tréilər] 예고편
the first trailer 첫 번째 예고편

**09 interesting** [íntərəstiŋ] 재미있는
an interesting movie 재미있는 영화

**10 festival** [féstəvəl] 축제
a film festival 영화제(영화 축제)

✎ 영어 단어를 완성하세요.

1   theater  극장

→   ⬜ heater  |  th ⬜ ate ⬜  |  ⬜ ⬜

2   movie  영화

→   ⬜ ovie  |  m ⬜ v ⬜ e  |  ⬜ ⬜

3   action  액션

→   a ⬜ tion  |  ⬜ c ⬜ ion  |  ⬜ ⬜

4   preview  시사회

→   pr ⬜ view  |  ⬜ re ⬜ iew  |  ⬜ ⬜

5   horror  공포

→   ho ⬜ ror  |  ⬜ orr ⬜ r  |  ⬜ ⬜

6   fantasy  상상, 공상

→   ⬜ antasy  |  f ⬜ nt ⬜ sy  |  ⬜ ⬜

7   mystery  미스터리

→   ⬜ ystery  |  m ⬜ st ⬜ ry  |  ⬜ ⬜

8   trailer  예고편

→   tr ⬜ iler  |  ⬜ rai ⬜ er  |  ⬜ ⬜

9   interesting  재미있는

→   in ⬜ eresting  |  ⬜ nter ⬜ sting  |  ⬜ ⬜

10  festival  축제

→   f ⬜ stival  |  ⬜ esti ⬜ al  |  ⬜ ⬜

# Practice

**A** 단어의 알맞은 뜻을 선으로 연결한 후, 빈칸에 단어를 직접 써보세요.

1 movie • • 축제 →
2 trailer • • 영화 →
3 fantasy • • 시사회 →
4 preview • • 상상, 공상 →
5 festival • • 예고편 →

**B** 우리말과 일치하도록 빈칸에 알맞은 단어를 보기 에서 찾아 쓰세요.

| 보기 | mystery | interesting | theater | horror | action |
|---|---|---|---|---|---|

1 극장에 가다 → go to the _____

2 공포 영화 → a _____ film

3 액션 영화 → an _____ movie

4 재미있는 영화 → an _____ movie

5 미스터리로 가득 차다 → be filled with _____

**C** 우리말을 참고해서 빈칸에 알맞은 단어를 골라 문장을 완성하세요.

1 When do they show the _____? 그들은 그 **영화**를 언제 상영하니?
( action / movie )

2 He canceled the press _____. 그는 그 기자 **시사회**를 취소했다.
( preview / mystery )

3 They showed the first _____. 그들은 첫 번째 **예고편**을 보여줬다.
( trailer / festival )

4 I don't want to see a _____ film. 나는 **공포** 영화를 보고 싶지 않다.
( horror / theater )

5 My child lives in a _____ world. 내 아이는 **상상** 세계에서 산다.
( fantasy / interesting )

**D** 우리말을 참고해서 알맞은 단어를 넣어 문장을 완성하세요.

1 I often go to the t_____. 나는 종종 **극장**에 간다.

2 The movie is filled with m_____. 그 영화는 **미스터리**로 가득 차 있다.

3 They really like a_____ movies. 그들은 정말로 **액션** 영화를 좋아한다.

4 It was a very i_____ movie. 그것은 매우 **재미있는** 영화였다.

5 Let's go to the film f_____. 그 영화제(영화 **축제**)에 가자.

# Politics 정치

**01 elect** [ilékt]
선출하다
elect him chairman 그를 의장으로 선출하다

**02 agree** [əgríː]
동의하다
agree to cooperate 협력하겠다고 동의하다

**03 Congress** [káŋɡrəs]
의회[국회]
run for Congress 의회에 출마하다

**04 freedom** [fríːdəm]
자유
keep our freedom 우리의 자유를 지키다

**05 equality** [ikwáləti]
평등
racial equality 인종 평등

**06 lead** [líːd]
이끌다
lead the club 그 클럽을 이끌다

**07 system** [sístəm]
제도, 체계
legal system 법률 제도

**08 follow** [fálou]
따르다
follow the rule 그 규칙을 따르다

**09 politics** [pálitiks]
정치
interested in politics 정치에 관심 있는

**10 impeach** [impíːtʃ]
탄핵하다
impeach the president 대통령을 탄핵하다

✎ 영어 단어를 완성하세요.

1  **elect** 선출하다
   →  el  ct        lec

2  **agree** 동의하다
   →  a  ree        gr  e

3  **Congress** 의회[국회]
   →  Con  ress      Co  gr  ss

4  **freedom** 자유
   →  fr  edom       ree  om

5  **equality** 평등
   →  quality        e  ua  ity

6  **lead** 이끌다
   →  l  ad         ea

7  **system** 제도, 체계
   →  ystem         sy  te

8  **follow** 따르다
   →  f  llow       oll  w

9  **politics** 정치
   →  olitics        p  liti  s

10  **impeach** 탄핵하다
   →  im  each       mpea  h

# ✎ Practice

**A** 단어의 알맞은 뜻을 선으로 연결한 후, 빈칸에 단어를 직접 써보세요.

1 freedom • • 동의하다 →  _____

2 agree • • 의회 [국회] →  _____

3 equality • • 자유 →  _____

4 impeach • • 평등 →  _____

5 Congress • • 탄핵하다 →  _____


**B** 우리말과 일치하도록 빈칸에 알맞은 단어를 보기 에서 찾아 쓰세요.

보기    elect    system    follow    politics    lead

1 법률 제도 → legal _____

2 그 규칙을 따르다 → _____ the rule

3 그를 의장으로 선출하다 → _____ him chairman

4 그 클럽을 이끌다 → _____ the club

5 정치에 관심 있는 → interested in _____

**C**  우리말을 참고해서 빈칸에 알맞은 단어를 골라 문장을 완성하세요.

**1**  He fought for racial _____.  그는 인종 **평등**을 위해 싸웠다.
( politics / equality )

**2**  We want to _____ him chairman.  우리는 그를 의장으로 **선출하기를** 원한다.
( elect / follow )

**3**  He wants to run for _____.  그는 **의회**에 출마하기를 원한다.
( system / Congress )

**4**  We do our best to keep our _____.  우리는 **자유**를 지키기 위해 최선을 다한다.
( freedom / equality )

**5**  Jane is going to _____ the club.  Jane이 그 클럽을 **이끌** 예정이다.
( agree / lead )

**D**  우리말을 참고해서 알맞은 단어를 넣어 문장을 완성하세요.

**1**  He  a _____ d  to cooperate fully.
그는 전적으로 협력하겠다고 **동의했다**.

**2**  We must  f _____  the rule.
우리는 그 규칙을 **따라야** 한다.

**3**  I'm not interested in  p _____ .
나는 **정치**에는 관심이 없다.

**4**  They vote on whether to  i _____  the president.
그들은 대통령을 **탄핵할지** 투표한다.

**5**  She read a book about the legal  s _____ .
그녀는 법률 **제도**에 대한 책을 읽었다.

## A 다음 영어 단어의 우리말 뜻을 쓰세요.

1  symptom  →  _____

2  fire station  →  _____

3  equality  →  _____

4  police office  →  _____

5  politics  →  _____

6  firefighter  →  _____

7  thief  →  _____

8  policeman  →  _____

9  movie  →  _____

10  treasure  →  _____

11  guidebook  →  _____

12  visitor  →  _____

13  clinic  →  _____

14  checkup  →  _____

## B 다음 우리말을 보고 영어표현을 완성하세요.

1  an old  p _____
고궁(오래된 궁전)

2  a  s _____  problem
심각한 문제

3  r _____  blood
왕실의 피

4  s _____  the forest
숲을 구하다

5  feel much  p _____
많은 고통을 느끼다

6  a _____  to cooperate
협력하겠다고 동의하다

7  get  s _____
병들다

8  legal  s _____
법률 제도

9  an  a _____  movie
액션 영화

10  f _____  the rule
그 규칙을 따르다

11  a  h _____  film
공포 영화

12  s _____  a car
차를 훔치다

13  in a  f _____  world
상상 세계에서

14  l _____  the club
그 클럽을 이끌다

## C 우리말과 같도록 괄호 안에서 알맞은 단어에 동그라미 하세요.

1 The kid set ( fire / thief ) to cars. 그 아이가 자동차들에 **불**을 질렀다.

2 I got a ( call / help ) to cry for help. 나는 도와달라는 **전화**를 받았다.

3 They display the old ( things / save ). 그들은 옛 **물건들**을 전시한다.

4 What an amazing ( movie / record ) it is! 그것은 놀라운 **기록**이구나!

5 He has to stay in the ( palace / hospital ). 그는 입원해야(**병원**에 머물러야) 한다.

6 I often go to the ( clinic / theater ). 나는 종종 **극장**에 간다.

7 It was a very ( interesting / horror ) movie. 그것은 매우 **재미있는** 영화였다.

8 He canceled the press ( action / preview ). 그는 그 기자 **시사회**를 취소했다.

## D 우리말과 같도록 다음 영어 문장을 완성하세요.

1 We do our best to keep our f_____. 우리는 **자유**를 지키기 위해 최선을 다한다.

2 We want to e_____ him chairman. 우리는 그를 의장으로 **선출하기를** 원한다.

3 A doctor is taking care of p_____s . 한 의사가 **환자들**을 돌보고 있다.

4 You have to get a flu s_____. 너는 독감 **주사**를 맞아야 한다.

5 We put out the fire with his h_____. 우리는 그의 **도움**으로 불을 껐다.

6 It is easy to catch the f_____ these days. 요즘은 **독감**에 걸리기 쉽다.

7 When do they visit the m_____? 그들은 **박물관**을 언제 방문하니?

8 The movie is filled with m_____. 그 영화는 **미스터리**로 가득 차 있다.

# Crime 범죄

**01 crime** [kraim] 범죄

violent crime 폭력 범죄

**02 law** [lɔ:] 법

obey the law 법을 지키다

**03 lawyer** [lɔ́:jər] 변호사

hire a lawyer 변호사를 선임하다

**04 sentence** [séntəns] 선고

pass sentence 선고를 내리다

**05 admit** [ədmít] 인정하다

admit the truth 진실을 인정하다

**06 judge** [dʒʌdʒ] 판사

before a judge 판사 앞에

**07 situation** [sìtʃuéiʃən] 상황

a confusing situation 혼란스러운 상황

**08 fact** [fækt] 사실

deny the fact 사실을 부인하다

**09 court** [kɔ:rt] 법원, 법정

appear in court 법원에 출두하다

**10 prison** [prízən] 감옥

in prison 감옥에서

✎ 영어 단어를 완성하세요.

1  **crime** 범죄
   → c ⬚ ime  |  ri ⬚ e  |  ⬚ ⬚

2  **law** 법
   → l ⬚ w  |  ⬚ a ⬚  |  ⬚ ⬚

3  **lawyer** 변호사
   → ⬚ awyer  |  l ⬚ wy ⬚ r  |  ⬚ ⬚

4  **sentence** 선고
   → sen ⬚ ence  |  ⬚ ent ⬚ nce  |  ⬚ ⬚

5  **admit** 인정하다
   → ad ⬚ it  |  ⬚ dmi ⬚  |  ⬚ ⬚

6  **judge** 판사
   → ⬚ udge  |  j ⬚ dg ⬚  |  ⬚ ⬚

7  **situation** 상황
   → situ ⬚ tion  |  si ⬚ ua ⬚ ion  |  ⬚ ⬚

8  **fact** 사실
   → f ⬚ ct  |  ⬚ ac ⬚  |  ⬚ ⬚

9  **court** 법원, 법정
   → c ⬚ urt  |  ⬚ our ⬚  |  ⬚ ⬚

10 **prison** 감옥
   → pr ⬚ son  |  ⬚ ri ⬚ on  |  ⬚ ⬚

# Practice

**A**  단어의 알맞은 뜻을 선으로 연결한 후, 빈칸에 단어를 직접 써보세요.

1  sentence  •            •  변호사    →  _____

2  judge  •               •  선고      →  _____

3  lawyer  •              •  인정하다  →  _____

4  situation  •           •  판사      →  _____

5  admit  •               •  상황      →  _____

**B**  우리말과 일치하도록 빈칸에 알맞은 단어를 보기 에서 찾아 쓰세요.

| 보기 | crime | prison | fact | law | court |
|---|---|---|---|---|---|

1  폭력 범죄        →  violent _____

2  감옥에서        →  in _____

3  사실을 부인하다  →  deny the _____

4  법원에 출두하다  →  appear in _____

5  법을 지키다      →  obey the _____

**C** 우리말을 참고해서 빈칸에 알맞은 단어를 골라 문장을 완성하세요.

1　It's no use denying the _____. 그 **사실**을 부인해도 소용없다.
（ fact / crime ）

2　She will appear in _____. 그녀는 **법원**에 출두할 것이다.
（ situation / court ）

3　We must obey the _____. 우리는 **법**을 지켜야 한다.
（ law / prison ）

4　He hired a good _____. 그는 훌륭한 **변호사**를 선임했다.
（ lawyer / judge ）

5　She didn't _____ the truth. 그녀는 그 진실을 **인정하지** 않았다.
（ admit / sentence ）

**D** 우리말을 참고해서 알맞은 단어를 넣어 문장을 완성하세요.

1　A judge passes s_____ on guilty persons.
판사는 죄 있는 자에게 **선고**를 내린다.

2　Violent c_____ is a serious problem.
폭력 **범죄**는 심각한 문제다.

3　Mr. Mandela spent 27 years in p_____.
만델라 대통령은 **감옥**에서 27년을 보냈다.

4　She finally stood before a j_____.
그녀는 마침내 **판사** 앞에 섰다.

5　They tried to end the confusing s_____.
그들은 그 혼란스러운 **상황**을 끝내려고 했다.

# Economy 경제

**01 money** [mʌ́ni]
돈
save some money 약간의 돈을 저축하다

**02 news** [njuːz]
소식, 뉴스
business news 기업 뉴스

**03 tax** [tæks]
세금
a tax on cigarettes 담뱃세(담배 세금)

**04 account** [əkáunt]
계좌
a bank account 은행 계좌

**05 economy** [ikánəmi]
경제
the world economy 세계 경제

**06 property** [prápərti]
재산
private property 사유 재산

**07 boom** [buːm]
호황
enjoy a boom 호황을 누리다

**08 recovery** [rikʌ́vəri]
회복
economic recovery 경제 회복

**09 exchange** [ikstʃéindʒ]
환전
an exchange rate 환율(환전 비율)

**10 piggy bank** [pigi bæŋk]
돼지 저금통
in a piggy bank 돼지 저금통에

✎ 영어 단어를 완성하세요.

1  **money** 돈
   → m　ney　　　　o　ey

2  **news** 소식, 뉴스
   → ne　s　　　　　ew

3  **tax** 세금
   → t　x　　　　　a

4  **account** 계좌
   → acc　unt　　　ccoun

5  **economy** 경제
   → eco　omy　　　cono　y

6  **property** 재산
   → 　roperty　　pr　per　y

7  **boom** 호황
   → b　om　　　　oo

8  **recovery** 회복
   → reco　ery　　ecover

9  **exchange** 환전
   → 　xchange　　ex　ha　ge

10 **piggy bank** 돼지 저금통
   → pigg　bank　　iggy　ank

# ✎ Practice

**A**  단어의 알맞은 뜻을 선으로 연결한 후, 빈칸에 단어를 직접 써보세요.

| | | | | | |
|---|---|---|---|---|---|
| 1 | piggy bank | • | • | 돈 | → |
| 2 | money | • | • | 돼지 저금통 | → |
| 3 | property | • | • | 소식, 뉴스 | → |
| 4 | news | • | • | 경제 | → |
| 5 | economy | • | • | 재산 | → |

**B**  우리말과 일치하도록 빈칸에 알맞은 단어를 보기 에서 찾아 쓰세요.

| 보기 | exchange | recovery | boom | account | tax |
|---|---|---|---|---|---|

1  은행 계좌   →   a bank _____

2  환율(환전 비율)   →   an _____ rate

3  담뱃세(담배 세금)   →   a _____ on cigarettes

4  경제 회복   →   economic _____

5  호황을 누리다   →   enjoy a _____

**C** 우리말을 참고해서 빈칸에 알맞은 단어를 골라 문장을 완성하세요.

1 I don't have a bank _____. 나는 은행 **계좌**가 없다.
( account / news )

2 What is the _____ rate? 환율(**환전 비율**)이 얼마인가요?
( tax / exchange )

3 It is a sign of economic _____. 그것은 경제 **회복** 징표다.
( recovery / boom )

4 They want to control private _____. 그들은 사유 **재산**을 통제하기를 원한다.
( economy / property )

5 We save some _____ every month. 우리는 매달 약간의 **돈**을 저축한다.
( money / tax )

**D** 우리말을 참고해서 알맞은 단어를 넣어 문장을 완성하세요.

1 My daughter keeps her money in the p_____.
내 딸은 **돼지 저금통**에 돈을 보관한다.

2 The government will cut a t_____ on cigarettes.
정부는 담뱃세(**담배 세금**)를 낮출 것이다.

3 It covers a variety of business n_____.
그것은 다양한 기업 **뉴스**를 다룬다.

4 Some countries control the world e_____.
몇몇 나라가 세계 **경제**를 지배한다.

5 The movie market is enjoying a b_____.
영화 시장은 **호황**을 누리고 있다.

# Prepositions 전치사

into  out of

| | | |
|---|---|---|
| 01 **before** [bifɔ́:r] 전에 | | 02 **after** [ǽftər] 후에 |
| before bed 자기 전에 | | after work 일이 끝난 후에 |

| | | |
|---|---|---|
| 03 **above** [əbʌ́v] 위에 | | 04 **below** [bilóu] 아래에 |
| above the clouds 구름 위에 | | below average 평균 아래에 |

| | | |
|---|---|---|
| 05 **behind** [biháind] 뒤에 | | 06 **in front of** [in frʌnt əv] 앞에 |
| behind the woman 그 여성 뒤에 | | in front of the mirror 거울 앞에 |

| | | |
|---|---|---|
| 07 **to** [tu:] ~로, ~을 향해 | | 08 **past** [pæst] ~을 지나서 |
| to the street 거리로 | | walk past me 나를 지나치다 |

| | | |
|---|---|---|
| 09 **into** [íntə] 안으로 | | 10 **out of** [aut əv] 밖으로 |
| into the water 물속으로 | | out of the burning house 불타는 집 밖으로 |

영어 단어를 완성하세요.

**1** before 전에

→ ⬜efore | b⬜for⬜ | ⬜⬜

**2** after 후에

→ a⬜ter | ⬜f⬜er | ⬜⬜

**3** above 위에

→ a⬜ove | ⬜bo⬜e | ⬜⬜

**4** below 아래에

→ ⬜elow | b⬜lo⬜ | ⬜⬜

**5** behind 뒤에

→ be⬜ind | ⬜ehin⬜ | ⬜⬜

**6** in front of 앞에

→ in⬜ront of | ⬜n front⬜f | ⬜⬜

**7** to ~로, ~을 향해

→ t⬜ | ⬜o | ⬜⬜

**8** past ~을 지나서

→ p⬜st | ⬜as⬜ | ⬜⬜

**9** into 안으로

→ in⬜o | i⬜t⬜ | ⬜⬜

**10** out of 밖으로

→ ou⬜of | ⬜ut⬜f | ⬜⬜

# Practice

**A** 단어의 알맞은 뜻을 선으로 연결한 후, 빈칸에 단어를 직접 써보세요.

1 out of • • 전에 →
2 after • • 밖으로 →
3 before • • 후에 →
4 in front of • • 뒤에 →
5 behind • • 앞에 →

**B** 우리말과 일치하도록 빈칸에 알맞은 단어를 보기 에서 찾아 쓰세요.

| 보기 | to | past | into | above | below |
|------|----|----|------|-------|-------|

1 구름 위에 → _____ the clouds

2 평균 아래에 → _____ average

3 거리로 → _____ the street

4 나를 지나치다 → walk _____ me

5 물속으로 → _____ the water

**C** 우리말을 참고해서 빈칸에 알맞은 단어를 골라 문장을 완성하세요.

1   She is standing _____ the mirror. 그녀는 그 거울 **앞에** 서 있다.
    ( in front of / past )

2   My school record is _____ average. 내 학교 성적은 평균 **아래**다.
    ( above / below )

3   A dog is running _____ the street. 개가 거리**로** 달려가고 있다.
    ( behind / to )

4   She always writes a diary _____ bed. 그녀는 자기 **전에** 항상 일기를 쓴다.
    ( after / before )

5   They ran _____ the burning house. 그들은 불타는 집 **밖으로** 뛰어나왔다.
    ( out of / into )

**D** 우리말을 참고해서 알맞은 단어를 넣어 문장을 완성하세요.

1   The women go to the beach  a_____ work.
    그 여자들은 일이 끝난 **후에** 해변에 간다.

2   A plane is flying  a_____ the clouds.
    비행기가 구름 **위를** 날고 있다.

3   There were many books  b_____ the woman.
    그 여성 **뒤에** 많은 책들이 있었다.

4   She walked  p_____ me without reacting.
    그녀는 반응 없이 나를 **지나**쳤다.

5   The children dived  i_____ the water.
    그 아이들이 물**속으로** 뛰어들었다.

# Antonyms 반의어

up

down

| 01 | **inside** [insáid] 안(쪽)에 |
|---|---|
| come inside 안에 들어오다 | |

| 02 | **outside** [àutsáid] 밖 [바깥]에 |
|---|---|
| go outside 밖에 나가다 | |

| 03 | **top** [tɑp] 맨 위 |
|---|---|
| the top of the hill 언덕 맨 위 | |

| 04 | **bottom** [bátəm] 맨 아래 |
|---|---|
| at the bottom 맨 아래에 | |

| 05 | **accept** [əksépt] 받아들이다 |
|---|---|
| accept his apology 그의 사과를 받아들이다 | |

| 06 | **reject** [ridʒékt] 거절하다 |
|---|---|
| reject the offer 그 제안을 거절하다 | |

| 07 | **more** [mɔːr] 더 많은 |
|---|---|
| more bread 더 많은 빵 | |

| 08 | **less** [les] 더 적은 |
|---|---|
| less time 더 적은 시간 | |

| 09 | **junior** [dʒúːnjər] 후배 |
|---|---|
| for his juniors 그의 후배들을 위해 | |

| 10 | **senior** [síːnjər] 선배 |
|---|---|
| follow the seniors 선배들을 따르다 | |

✎ 영어 단어를 완성하세요.

1　inside 안(쪽)에
→ in___ide　　___nsi___e　　[___][___]

2　outside 밖[바깥]에
→ ou___side　　___ut___ide　　[___][___]

3　top 맨 위
→ t___p　　___o___　　[___][___]

4　bottom 맨 아래
→ ___ottom　　b___tto___　　[___][___]

5　accept 받아들이다
→ acc___pt　　___cce___t　　[___][___]

6　reject 거절하다
→ re___ect　　r___je___t　　[___][___]

7　more 더 많은
→ ___ore　　m___r___　　[___][___]

8　less 더 적은
→ le___s　　___ss　　[___][___]

9　junior 후배
→ ___unior　　j___nio___　　[___][___]

10　senior 선배
→ ___enior　　s___ni___r　　[___][___]

# ✎ Practice

**A** 단어의 알맞은 뜻을 선으로 연결한 후, 빈칸에 단어를 직접 써보세요.

| 1 | junior | • | | • | 안(쪽)에 | → | |
| 2 | senior | • | | • | 후배 | → | |
| 3 | inside | • | | • | 선배 | → | |
| 4 | outside | • | | • | 받아들이다 | → | |
| 5 | accept | • | | • | 밖[바깥]에 | → | |

**B** 우리말과 일치하도록 빈칸에 알맞은 단어를 보기 에서 찾아 쓰세요.

| 보기 | more | top | bottom | reject | less |

1 더 많은 빵 → _____ bread

2 더 적은 시간 → _____ time

3 언덕 맨 위 → the _____ of the hill

4 맨 아래에 → at the _____

5 그 제안을 거절하다 → _____ the offer

**C** 우리말을 참고해서 빈칸에 알맞은 단어를 골라 문장을 완성하세요.

1 He has some advice for his ＿＿＿＿＿＿＿. 그는 **후배들**을 위해 몇 가지 충고를 한다.
　　　　　　　　　　　　　　　( seniors / juniors )

2 The book is at the ＿＿＿＿＿＿＿. 그 책은 **맨 아래**에 있다.
　　　　　　　　　　　( top / bottom )

3 The company has to ＿＿＿＿＿＿＿ the offer. 그 회사는 그 제안을 **거절해야** 한다.
　　　　　　　　　　( reject / accept )

4 She needs to bake ＿＿＿＿＿＿＿ bread. 그녀는 **더 많은** 빵을 구워야 한다.
　　　　　　　　　　( more / less )

5 The students follow the ＿＿＿＿＿＿＿. 그 학생들은 **선배들**을 따른다.
　　　　　　　　　　　( seniors / juniors )

**D** 우리말을 참고해서 알맞은 단어를 넣어 문장을 완성하세요.

1 Come i＿＿＿＿＿＿ and get warm.
**안에** 들어와 몸을 녹여라.

2 We climb to the t＿＿＿＿＿＿ of the hill.
우리는 언덕 **맨 위**까지 올라간다.

3 Jane decided to a＿＿＿＿＿＿ his apology.
Jane은 그의 사과를 **받아들이기로** 결심했다.

4 She spends l＿＿＿＿＿＿ time exercising.
그녀는 운동하는 데 **더 적은** 시간을 쓴다.

5 My mom can't go o＿＿＿＿＿＿ today.
나의 엄마는 오늘 **밖에** 나갈 수 없다.

# Verb Phrases 동사구

**01**
## turn on
[təːrn ən]
켜다

turn on **a fan** 선풍기를 켜다

**02**
## turn off
[təːrn ɔːf]
끄다

turn off **a light** 불[전등]을 끄다

**03**
## climb up
[klaim ʌp]
올라가다

climb up **a hill** 언덕을 오르다

**04**
## climb down
[klaim dáun]
내려오다

climb down **a tree** 나무에서 내려오다

**05**
## get on
[get ən]
(탈것을) 타다

get on **a bus** 버스에 타다

**06**
## get off
[get ɔːf]
(탈것에서) 내리다

**where to** get off 어디서 내려야 하는지

**07**
## turn down
[təːrn dáun]
약하게 하다

turn down **the heat** 불을 줄이다(약하게 하다)

**08**
## turn up
[təːrn ʌp]
크게 하다

turn up **the volume** 볼륨을 크게 하다

**09**
## put on
[put ən]
입다

put on **a coat** 코트를 입다

**10**
## take off
[teik ɔːf]
벗다

take off **shoes** 신발을 벗다

영어 단어를 완성하세요.

**1** turn on 켜다

→ tur___ on   ___urn ___n   [ ___ | ___ ]

**2** turn off 끄다

→ ___urn off   tur___ of___   [ ___ | ___ ]

**3** climb up 올라가다

→ climb ___p   c___imb u___   [ ___ | ___ ]

**4** climb down 내려오다

→ ___limb down   cli___b do___n   [ ___ | ___ ]

**5** get on (탈것을) 타다

→ g___t on   ___et ___n   [ ___ | ___ ]

**6** get off (탈것에서) 내리다

→ ___et off   ge___ of___   [ ___ | ___ ]

**7** turn down 약하게 하다

→ tur___ down   t___rn d___wn   [ ___ | ___ ]

**8** turn up 크게 하다

→ t___rn up   ___urn ___p   [ ___ | ___ ]

**9** put on 입다

→ p___t on   ___ut ___n   [ ___ | ___ ]

**10** take off 벗다

→ ta___e off   ___ake ___ff   [ ___ | ___ ]

# Practice

## A 단어의 알맞은 뜻을 선으로 연결한 후, 빈칸에 단어를 직접 써보세요.

| | | | |
|---|---|---|---|
| 1 | turn on • | • (탈것을) 타다 | → [ ] |
| 2 | climb down • | • 켜다 | → [ ] |
| 3 | turn down • | • 올라가다 | → [ ] |
| 4 | get on • | • 내려오다 | → [ ] |
| 5 | climb up • | • 약하게 하다 | → [ ] |

## B 우리말과 일치하도록 빈칸에 알맞은 단어를 보기 에서 찾아 쓰세요.

| 보기 | turn up | get off | turn off | put on | take off |
|---|---|---|---|---|---|

1  코트를 입다   → _____ a coat

2  신발을 벗다   → _____ shoes

3  불[전등]을 끄다   → _____ a light

4  어디서 내려야 하는지   → where to _____

5  볼륨을 크게 하다   → _____ the volume

**C** 우리말을 참고해서 빈칸에 알맞은 단어를 골라 문장을 완성하세요.

1 May I _____ the fan? 내가 그 선풍기를 **켜도** 될까요?
( turn on / turn up )

2 The cat _____ the tree slowly. 그 고양이는 그 나무에서 천천히 **내려온다.**
( climbs up / climbs down )

3 I saw him _____ the bus. 나는 그가 버스에 **타는** 것을 보았다.
( get on / put on )

4 Let me know where to _____. 어디서 **내려야** 하는지 알려 주세요.
( take off / get off )

5 She has to _____ the heat. 그녀는 불을 줄여야(**약하게 해야**) 한다.
( turn off / turn down )

**D** 우리말을 참고해서 알맞은 단어를 넣어 문장을 완성하세요.

1 Would you  t _____ the volume?
볼륨 좀 **크게 해** 줄래?

2 It is good to  p _____ a coat.
코트를 **입는** 것이 좋다.

3 They don't have to  t _____ their shoes.
그들은 신발을 **벗을** 필요가 없다.

4 My friends decided to  c _____ the hill.
내 친구들은 그 언덕을 **오르기로** 결심했다.

5 You have to  t _____ the lights before going out.
너는 나가기 전에 불[전등]을 **꺼야** 한다.

## A 다음 영어 단어의 우리말 뜻을 쓰세요.

1 put on → _____
2 crime → _____
3 take off → _____
4 lawyer → _____
5 news → _____
6 before → _____
7 tax → _____
8 after → _____
9 in front of → _____
10 turn off → _____
11 out of → _____
12 climb up → _____
13 turn on → _____
14 climb down → _____

## B 다음 우리말을 보고 영어표현을 완성하세요.

1 r_____ the offer
제안을 거절하다

2 the world e_____
세계 경제

3 in p_____
감옥에서

4 enjoy a b_____
호황을 누리다

5 a_____ his apology
그의 사과를 받아들이다

6 b_____ the woman
그 여성 뒤에

7 before a j_____
판사 앞에

8 t_____ the street
거리로

9 appear in c_____
법원에 출두하다

10 walk p_____ me
나를 지나치다

11 economic r_____
경제 회복

12 the t_____ of the hill
언덕 맨 위

13 i_____ the water
물속으로

14 at the b_____
맨 아래에

**C** 우리말과 같도록 괄호 안에서 알맞은 단어에 동그라미 하세요.

1    She didn't ( admit / reject ) the truth. 그녀는 그 진실을 **인정하지** 않았다.

2    It's no use denying the ( news / fact ). 그 **사실**을 부인해도 소용없다.

3    We must obey the ( prison / law ). 우리는 **법**을 지켜야 한다.

4    I don't have a bank ( accept / account ). 나는 은행 **계좌**가 없다.

5    Let me know where to ( get on / get off ). 어디서 **내려야** 하는지 알려 주세요.

6    What is the ( money / exchange ) rate? 환율(**환전** 비율)이 얼마인가요?

7    Come ( inside / outside ) and get warm. **안에** 들어와서 몸을 녹여라.

8    Would you ( turn up / turn on ) the volume? 볼륨 좀 **크게 해** 줄래?


**D** 우리말과 같도록 다음 영어 문장을 완성하세요.

1    She spends l_____ time exercising. 그녀는 운동하는 데 **더 적은** 시간을 쓴다.

2    I saw him g_____ the bus. 나는 그가 버스에 **타는** 것을 보았다.

3    She has to t_____ the heat. 그녀는 불을 줄여야(**약하게 해야**) 한다.

4    We save some m_____ every month. 우리는 매달 약간의 **돈을** 저축한다.

5    My school record is b_____ average. 내 학교 성적은 평균 **아래다**.

6    A plane is flying a_____ the clouds. 비행기가 구름 **위를** 날고 있다.

7    She needs to bake m_____ bread. 그녀는 **더 많은** 빵을 구워야 한다.

8    My mom can't go o_____ today. 나의 엄마는 오늘 **밖에** 나갈 수 없다.

# ANSWERS
정답

# ANSWERS 정답

## Unit 01
pp.14-15

**A**
1 학생 → pupil
2 반 친구 → classmate
3 가르치다 → teach
4 교장 → principal
5 구내식당 → cafeteria

**B**
1 absent
2 present
3 education
4 semester
5 schedule

**C**
1 absent
2 teaches
3 schedule
4 classmate
5 principal

**D**
1 pupils
2 cafeteria
3 present
4 semester
5 education

## Unit 02
pp.18-19

**A**
1 미술 → art
2 음악 → music
3 레슨, 수업 → lesson
4 과학 → science
5 역사 → history

**B**
1 learn
2 tutor
3 understand
4 curriculum
5 subject

**C**
1 science
2 subject
3 lessons
4 art
5 understand

**D**
1 music
2 history
3 tutor
4 curriculum
5 learn

## Unit 03
pp.22-23

**A**
1 낙제하다 → fail
2 합격하다 → pass
3 쉬운 → easy
4 점수 → score
5 답, 해답 → answer

**B**
1 finish
2 grades
3 cheat
4 difficult
5 examination

**C**
1 grades
2 fail
3 cheated
4 answer
5 easy

**D**
1 score
2 pass
3 difficult
4 finish
5 examination

## Unit 04
pp.26-27

**A**
1 공부하다 → study
2 복습하다 → review
3 그룹, 모임 → group
4 충고 → advice
5 변명 → excuse

**B**
1 effort
2 example
3 homework
4 problem
5 explain

**C**
1 homework
2 groups
3 study
4 example
5 advice

**D**
1 review
2 explain
3 problem
4 effort
5 excuse

## Unit 05
pp.30-31

**A**
1 분필 → chalk
2 앨범 → album
3 스테이플러 → stapler
4 폴더 → folder
5 나침반 → compass

**B**
1 clipboard
2 scissors
3 sketchbook
4 stationery
5 highlighter

**C**
1 chalk
2 clipboard
3 sketchbook
4 scissors
5 stationery

**D**
1 album
2 folder
3 stapler
4 compass
5 highlighter

## Review

pp.32-33

**A** 1 미술 2 분필 3 학생
4 스테이플러 5 결석한 6 교장
7 숙제 8 반 친구 9 역사
10 형광펜 11 학기 12 가위
13 어려운 14 교육

**B** 1 album 2 easy 3 teach
4 learn 5 study 6 compass
7 pass 8 effort 9 grades
10 answer 11 cheat 12 finish
13 tutor 14 explain

**C** 1 science 2 example 3 fail
4 score 5 lessons 6 present
7 examination 8 excuse

**D** 1 advice 2 subject 3 music
4 folder 5 review 6 cafeteria
7 understand 8 problem

## Unit 06

pp.36-37

**A** 1 기다리다 → wait 2 잊다 → forget
3 여가 → leisure 4 방학 → vacation
5 기억하다 → remember

**B** 1 planner 2 during 3 wonderful
4 country 5 participate

**C** 1 forget 2 wonderful 3 wait
4 vacation 5 participate

**D** 1 country 2 remember 3 planner
4 leisure 5 during

## Unit 07

pp.40-41

**A** 1 (꽃을) 꺾다 → pick 2 소풍 → picnic
3 대회 → contest 4 바구니 → basket
5 활동 → activity

**B** 1 hurry 2 leave 3 special
4 happen 5 volunteer

**C** 1 picnic 2 hurry 3 happened
4 special 5 activity

**D** 1 pick 2 contest 3 leave
4 volunteer 5 basket

## Unit 08

pp.44-45

**A** 1 경기, 시합 → match 2 막다 → block
3 패자 → loser 4 응원하다 → cheer
5 승자 → winner

**B** 1 field 2 whistle 3 playground
4 medal 5 march

**C** 1 winner 2 field 3 blocked
4 march 5 medal

**D** 1 cheer 2 loser 3 playground
4 match 5 whistle

## Unit 09

pp.48-49

**A** 1 입학하다 → enter 2 자랑스러운 → proud
3 우등, 명예 → honor 4 기억 → memory
5 졸업하다 → graduate

**B** 1 beginning 2 university 3 elementary
4 kindergarten 5 congratulation

**C** 1 entered 2 elementary 3 honor
4 kindergarten 5 congratulation

**D** 1 proud 2 university 3 beginning
4 graduate 5 memory

## Unit 10
pp.52-53

A 1 깨끗한 → tidy  2 닦다 → wipe
3 지저분한 → messy  4 비우다, 빈 → empty
5 고치다 → repair

B 1 dusty  2 polish  3 cleanup
4 restroom  5 post

C 1 post  2 wipe  3 cleanup
4 restroom  5 tidy

D 1 repair  2 empty  3 messy
4 dusty  5 polish

## Review
pp.54-55

A 1 바구니  2 자랑스러운  3 잊다
4 일어나다  5 ~ 동안  6 청소
7 화장실  8 계획표  9 특별한
10 호루라기  11 대학  12 활동
13 방학  14 지원자

B 1 pick  2 tidy  3 enter
4 medal  5 contest  6 block
7 post  8 empty  9 leave
10 memory  11 picnic  12 messy
13 match  14 wipe

C 1 country  2 winner  3 graduate
4 remember  5 elementary  6 wonderful
7 honor  8 leisure

D 1 wait  2 field  3 dusty
4 loser  5 cheer  6 polish
7 hurry  8 repair

## Unit 11
pp.58-59

A 1 잘하는 → good  2 못하는 → poor
3 인기 있는 → popular  4 표현하다 → express
5 공연하다 → perform

B 1 classical  2 concert  3 imagine
4 audience  5 entertain

C 1 poor  2 express  3 classical
4 audience  5 perform

D 1 good  2 concert  3 entertain
4 popular  5 imagine

## Unit 12
pp.62-63

A 1 절하다 → bow  2 방안, 생각 → idea
3 즐거운 → merry  4 존경하다 → respect
5 아주 멋진 → terrific

B 1 holiday  2 decorate  3 touching
4 impressive  5 traditional

C 1 terrific  2 holiday  3 impressive
4 decorate  5 traditional

D 1 idea  2 merry  3 respect
4 touching  5 bow

## Unit 13
pp.66-67

A 1 직업, 직장 → job  2 고용하다 → hire
3 일, 직무 → task  4 사무실 → office
5 회사 → company

B 1 business  2 artist  3 pilot
4 soldier  5 counselor

C 1 task  2 pilot  3 hire
4 business  5 counselor

D 1 job  2 artist  3 office
4 soldier  5 company

## Unit 14
pp.70-71

A 1 장소, 곳 → place  2 호텔 → hotel
  3 제과점 → bakery  4 도서관 → library
  5 서점 → bookstore

B 1 village  2 station  3 town
  4 located  5 airport

C 1 village  2 located  3 bookstore
  4 station  5 bakery

D 1 hotel  2 town  3 place
  4 airport  5 library

## Unit 15
pp.74-75

A 1 복잡한, 바쁜 → busy  2 국가 → nation
  3 해외에 → abroad  4 수도 → capital
  5 건물 → building

B 1 local  2 facility  3 crowded
  4 metropolis  5 outskirt

C 1 nations  2 facility  3 crowded
  4 building  5 outskirt

D 1 local  2 busy  3 abroad
  4 capital  5 metropolis

## Review
pp.76-77

A 1 나라  2 상상하다  3 공항
  4 즐겁게 하다  5 도서관  6 서점
  7 휴일  8 회사  9 인기 있는
  10 상담사  11 공연하다  12 시설
  13 존경하다  14 인상적인

B 1 job  2 task  3 idea
  4 pilot  5 hotel  6 town
  7 busy  8 bow  9 hire
  10 abroad  11 concert  12 bakery
  13 place  14 building

C 1 poor  2 soldier  3 business
  4 station  5 located  6 decorate
  7 touching  8 traditional

D 1 good  2 local  3 merry
  4 office  5 village  6 crowded
  7 capital  8 express

## Unit 16
pp.80-81

A 1 전쟁 → war  2 세계, 세상 → world
  3 인간[인류]의 → human  4 평화 → peace
  5 빙산 → iceberg

B 1 polar  2 island  3 erupt
  4 global  5 continent

C 1 war  2 island  3 erupted
  4 polar  5 global

D 1 human  2 peace  3 continent
  4 iceberg  5 world

## Unit 17
pp.84-85

A 1 신부 → bride  2 결혼하다 → marry
  3 신랑 → groom  4 이혼 → divorce
  5 청혼하다 → propose

B 1 single  2 couple  3 date
  4 wedding  5 honeymoon

C 1 single  2 date  3 marry
  4 groom  5 proposed

D 1 divorce  2 bride  3 wedding
  4 honeymoon  5 couple

## Unit 18
pp.88-89

**A**
1 버리다 → dump    2 종이 → paper
3 파괴하다 → destroy    4 보호하다 → protect
5 재활용하다 → recycle

**B**
1 issue    2 plastic    3 pollution
4 harm    5 environment

**C**
1 issue    2 plastic    3 dumped
4 destroyed    5 pollution

**D**
1 protect    2 recycle    3 paper
4 environment    5 harm

## Unit 19
pp.92-93

**A**
1 운이 좋은 → lucky    2 고생하다 → suffer
3 결과 → result    4 홍수, 범람 → flood
5 끔찍한 → terrible

**B**
1 fall    2 crash    3 cause
4 accident    5 earthquake

**C**
1 terrible    2 crashed    3 flood
4 result    5 accident

**D**
1 fall    2 lucky    3 suffer
4 caused    5 earthquake

## Unit 20
pp.96-97

**A**
1 죄, 죄악 → sin    2 신 → god
3 삶, 생명 → life    4 죽음 → death
5 사원, 절 → temple

**B**
1 pray    2 believe    3 forgive
4 create    5 religions

**C**
1 gods    2 temple    3 forgive
4 death    5 religions

**D**
1 pray    2 sin    3 believe
4 life    5 created

## Review
pp.98-99

**A**
1 섬    2 신랑    3 평화
4 죽음    5 결과    6 용서하다
7 창조하다    8 믿다    9 파괴하다
10 사고    11 빙산    12 오염
13 지진    14 환경

**B**
1 date    2 war    3 harm
4 dump    5 fall    6 pray
7 bride    8 world    9 polar
10 paper    11 single    12 erupt
13 couple    14 temple

**C**
1 gods    2 terrible    3 global
4 plastic    5 recycle    6 divorce
7 continent    8 caused

**D**
1 life    2 sin    3 marry
4 issue    5 flood    6 protect
7 lucky    8 suffer

## Unit 21
pp.102-103

**A**
1 동물 → animal    2 먹이[사냥감] → prey
3 야생(의) → wild    4 살다 → live
5 왕국 → kingdom

**B**
1 raise    2 species    3 feed
4 beast    5 domestic

**C**
1 animals    2 feed    3 domestic
4 raise    5 beast

**D**
1 live    2 wild    3 prey
4 kingdom    5 species

## Unit 22
pp.106-107

A 1 가시 → thorn  2 허브 → herb
  3 빽빽한 → dense  4 자라다 → grow
  5 다르다 → vary

B 1 native  2 stem  3 roots
  4 water  5 bloom

C 1 herbs  2 water  3 thorn
  4 roots  5 bloom

D 1 grow  2 native  3 vary
  4 dense  5 stem

## Unit 23
pp.110-111

A 1 해충 → pest  2 이로운 → helpful
  3 독 → poison  4 곤충 → insect
  5 낳다 → lay

B 1 harmful  2 spray  3 attack
  4 caterpillar  5 hatch

C 1 insects  2 hatch  3 harmful
  4 lay  5 pests

D 1 poison  2 attack  3 caterpillar
  4 helpful  5 spray

## Unit 24
pp.114-115

A 1 날씨 → weather  2 햇빛, 햇살 → sunshine
  3 소나기 → shower  4 맑은 → clear
  5 따뜻한 → warm

B 1 forecast  2 thunder  3 cloudy
  4 cool  5 lightning

C 1 warm  2 cool  3 lightning
  4 thunder  5 weather

D 1 forecast  2 sunshine  3 cloudy
  4 clear  5 shower

## Unit 25
pp.118-119

A 1 신호 → signal  2 보행자 → pedestrian
  3 교통 → traffic  4 횡단보도 → crosswalk
  5 범퍼 → bumper

B 1 street  2 speed  3 parking
  4 tow  5 way

C 1 traffic  2 speed  3 crosswalk
  4 signal  5 parking

D 1 tow  2 street  3 way
  4 bumper  5 pedestrian

## Review
pp.120-121

A 1 낳다  2 종류, (생물) 종  3 뿌리다
  4 뿌리  5 애벌레  6 자라다
  7 따뜻한  8 해충  9 맑은
  10 번개  11 길  12 소나기
  13 허브  14 천둥

B 1 raise  2 sunshine  3 live
  4 forecast  5 stem  6 crosswalk
  7 vary  8 tow  9 harmful
  10 parking  11 cloudy  12 wild
  13 kingdom  14 beast

C 1 native  2 thorn  3 insects
  4 attack  5 hatch  6 cool
  7 traffic  8 signal

D 1 prey  2 feed  3 water
  4 bloom  5 dense  6 poison
  7 street  8 speed

## Unit 26 pp.124-125

**A**
1 승객 → passenger
2 지하의 → underground
3 갈아타다 → transfer
4 지역 → area
5 운전사 → driver

**B**
1 subway
2 fare
3 ticket
4 broken
5 highway

**C**
1 subway
2 passengers
3 driver
4 transfer
5 ticket

**D**
1 broken
2 underground
3 highway
4 fares
5 area

## Unit 27 pp.128-129

**A**
1 디지털의 → digital
2 충전하다 → charge
3 (과학) 기술 → technology
4 기계 → machine
5 발명하다 → invent

**B**
1 energy
2 creative
3 basic
4 develop
5 switch

**C**
1 invented
2 technology
3 machine
4 charge
5 digital

**D**
1 energy
2 creative
3 develop
4 switch
5 basic

## Unit 28 pp.132-133

**A**
1 계곡 → valley
2 우주비행사 → astronaut
3 우주선 → spaceship
4 행성 → planet
5 태평양 → Pacific

**B**
1 space
2 earth
3 forest
4 ocean
5 desert

**C**
1 space
2 astronaut
3 valleys
4 Pacific
5 earth

**D**
1 forest
2 ocean
3 planet
4 desert
5 spaceship

## Unit 29 pp.136-137

**A**
1 잘 익힌 → well-done
2 주문하다 → order
3 메뉴 → menu
4 만들다 → make
5 식당 → restaurant

**B**
1 reserve
2 chef
3 medium
4 tip
5 waiter

**C**
1 make
2 medium
3 restaurant
4 menu
5 order

**D**
1 reserve
2 waiter
3 chefs
4 well-done
5 tip

## Unit 30 pp.140-141

**A**
1 엽서 → postcard
2 우편 번호 → zip code
3 소포 → package
4 봉투 → envelope
5 우체국 → post office

**B**
1 direct
2 regular
3 airmail
4 form
5 express

**C**
1 post office
2 envelope
3 airmail
4 postcard
5 zip code

**D**
1 package
2 form
3 express
4 regular
5 direct

## Review pp.142-143

**A**
1 요금
2 메뉴
3 고장 난
4 엽서
5 개발하다
6 직접적인
7 행성
8 소포
9 잘 익힌
10 속달의
11 우체국
12 지하의
13 우편 번호
14 식당

B   1 basic          2 ticket         3 space
    4 creative       5 spaceship      6 reserve
    7 ocean          8 tip            9 desert
    10 form          11 airmail       12 subway
    13 energy        14 highway

C   1 area           2 invented       3 forest
    4 waiter         5 order          6 make
    7 envelope       8 transfer

D   1 driver         2 machine        3 charge
    4 digital        5 switch         6 earth
    7 valleys        8 chefs

D   1 visitors       2 guidebooks     3 treasure
    4 exhibition     5 palace

## Unit 33                                    pp.154-155

A   1 진료소 → clinic        2 고통 → pain
    3 아픈, 병든 → sick      4 환자 → patient
    5 증상 → symptom

B   1 shot           2 checkup        3 serious
    4 flu            5 hospital

C   1 patients       2 clinics        3 shot
    4 pain           5 sick

D   1 hospital       2 flu            3 symptom
    4 checkup        5 serious

## Unit 31                                    pp.146-147

A   1 소방서 → fire station    2 경찰서 → police office
    3 도둑 → thief            4 소방관 → firefighter
    5 훔치다 → steal

B   1 policeman      2 fire           3 save
    4 call           5 help

C   1 saved          2 fire station   3 steal
    4 police office  5 fire

D   1 call           2 help           3 thief
    4 firefighter    5 policeman

## Unit 34                                    pp.158-159

A   1 영화 → movie           2 예고편 → trailer
    3 상상, 공상 → fantasy     4 시사회 → preview
    5 축제 → festival

B   1 theater        2 horror         3 action
    4 interesting    5 mystery

C   1 movie          2 preview        3 trailer
    4 horror         5 fantasy

D   1 theater        2 mystery        3 action
    4 interesting    5 festival

## Unit 32                                    pp.150-151

A   1 박물관 → museum        2 물건 → thing
    3 보물 → treasure        4 방문객 → visitor
    5 뛰어난 → outstanding

B   1 palace         2 royal          3 guidebook
    4 exhibition     5 record

C   1 record         2 Royal          3 outstanding
    4 things         5 museum

## Unit 35                                    pp.162-163

A   1 자유 → freedom         2 동의하다 → agree
    3 평등 → equality        4 탄핵하다 → impeach
    5 의회[국회] → Congress

B   1 system         2 follow         3 elect
    4 lead           5 politics

C 1 equality　　2 elect　　　3 Congress
4 freedom　　5 lead

D 1 agreed　　　2 follow　　　3 politics
4 impeach　　 5 system

## Review

pp.164-165

A 1 증상　　　　2 소방서　　　3 평등
4 경찰서　　　5 정치　　　　6 소방관
7 도둑　　　　8 경찰관　　　9 영화
10 보물　　　 11 안내서　　 12 방문객
13 진료소　　 14 건강검진

B 1 palace　　　2 serious　　　3 royal
4 save　　　　5 pain　　　　6 agree
7 sick　　　　8 system　　　9 action
10 follow　　 11 horror　　 12 steal
13 fantasy　　14 lead

C 1 fire　　　　2 call　　　　3 things
4 record　　　5 hospital　　6 theater
7 interesting　8 preview

D 1 freedom　　2 elect　　　　3 patients
4 shot　　　　5 help　　　　6 flu
7 museum　　 8 mystery

## Unit 36
pp.168-169

A 1 선고 → sentence　　2 판사 → judge
3 변호사 → lawyer　　4 상황 → situation
5 인정하다 → admit

B 1 crime　　　2 prison　　　3 fact
4 court　　　5 law

C 1 fact　　　　2 court　　　　3 law
4 lawyer　　　5 admit

D 1 sentence　　2 crime　　　3 prison
4 judge　　　5 situation

## Unit 37
pp.172-173

A 1 돼지 저금통 → piggy bank　2 돈 → money
3 재산 → property　　4 소식, 뉴스 → news
5 경제 → economy

B 1 account　　2 exchange　　3 tax
4 recovery　　5 boom

C 1 account　　2 exchange　　3 recovery
4 property　　5 money

D 1 piggy bank　2 tax　　　　3 news
4 economy　　5 boom

## Unit 38
pp.176-177

A 1 밖으로 → out of　　2 후에 → after
3 전에 → before　　　4 앞에 → in front of
5 뒤에 → behind

B 1 above　　　2 below　　　3 to
4 past　　　　5 into

C 1 in front of　2 below　　　3 to
4 before　　　5 out of

D 1 after　　　2 above　　　3 behind
4 past　　　　5 into

## Unit 39
pp.180-181

A 1 후배 → junior　　2 선배 → senior
3 안(쪽)에 → inside　　4 밖[바깥]에 → outside
5 받아들이다 → accept

B 1 more　　　2 less　　　　3 top
4 bottom　　　5 reject

C 1 juniors　　2 bottom　　　3 reject
4 more　　　5 seniors

D 1 inside　　　2 top　　　　3 accept
4 less　　　　5 outside

## Unit 40

pp.184-185

A
1 켜다 → turn on
2 내려오다 → climb down
3 약하게 하다 → turn down
4 (탈것을) 타다 → get on
5 올라가다 → climb up

B
1 put on    2 take off    3 turn off
4 get off    5 turn up

C
1 turn on    2 climbs down    3 get on
4 get off    5 turn down

D
1 turn up    2 put on    3 take off
4 climb up    5 turn off

## Review

pp.186-187

A
1 입다    2 범죄    3 벗다
4 변호사    5 소식, 뉴스    6 전에
7 세금    8 후에    9 앞에
10 끄다    11 밖으로    12 올라가다
13 켜다    14 내려오다

B
1 reject    2 economy    3 prison
4 boom    5 accept    6 behind
7 judge    8 to    9 court
10 past    11 recovery    12 top
13 into    14 bottom

C
1 admit    2 fact    3 law
4 account    5 get off    6 exchange
7 inside    8 turn up

D
1 less    2 get on    3 turn down
4 money    5 below    6 above
7 more    8 outside

# Memo

Longman

# Vocabulary

## MENTOR

Social Words

## JOY

WORKBOOK

3

| 보기 | pupil | teach | absent | present | principal |
|------|-------|-------|--------|---------|-----------|
| | schedule | semester | classmate | cafeteria | education |

**A** 우리말 뜻을 보고 알맞은 단어를 보기 에서 찾아 쓰세요.

1 반 친구 → 
2 가르치다 → 
3 참석한 → 
4 결석한 → 
5 교장 → 
6 학생 → 
7 학기 → 
8 시간표 → 
9 교육 → 
10 구내식당 → 

**B** 우리말을 보고 보기 에서 알맞은 단어를 찾아 영어표현을 완성하세요.

1 영어를 가르치다 → _____ English

2 대부분의 학생들 → most _____ s

3 학교에 결석한 → _____ from school

4 가을 학기 → the fall _____

5 파티에 참석한 → _____ at the party

6 수업 시간표 → a class _____

7 여교장 → a lady _____

8 전학생(새 반 친구) → a new _____

9 구내식당에서 → in a _____

10 교육을 받다 → get an _____

| 보기 | subject | science | music | history | art |
| --- | --- | --- | --- | --- | --- |
| | learn | understand | lesson | curriculum | tutor |

**A** 우리말 뜻을 보고 알맞은 단어를 보기 에서 찾아 쓰세요.

1 음악 → _____ 　 2 미술 → _____

3 역사 → _____ 　 4 과학 → _____

5 과목 → _____ 　 6 레슨, 수업 → _____

7 배우다 → _____ 　 8 이해하다 → _____

9 가정교사 → _____ 　 10 교육과정 → _____

**B** 우리말을 보고 보기 에서 알맞은 단어를 찾아 영어표현을 완성하세요.

1 현대 미술 → modern _____

2 역사책 → a _____ book

3 음악 수업 → _____ class

4 과학 선생님 → a _____ teacher

5 내가 가장 좋아하는 과목 → my favorite _____

6 수학 가정교사 → a math _____

7 레슨을 받다 → take _____ s

8 사용법을 배우다 → _____ to use

9 이해하기 어려운 → hard to _____

10 학교 교육과정 → the school _____

| 보기 | | | | | |
|---|---|---|---|---|---|
| | pass | fail | answer | examination | score |
| | grade | easy | difficult | cheat | finish |

**A** 우리말 뜻을 보고 알맞은 단어를 보기 에서 찾아 쓰세요.

1 쉬운 → 　　　　　　　　2 답, 해답 →

3 점수 → 　　　　　　　　4 합격하다 →

5 낙제하다 → 　　　　　　6 성적, 학년 →

7 어려운 → 　　　　　　　8 끝내다 →

9 시험 → 　　　　　　　　10 부정행위 하다 →

**B** 우리말을 보고 보기 에서 알맞은 단어를 찾아 영어표현을 완성하세요.

1 답안지 → an ＿＿＿＿＿＿＿＿ sheet

2 점수를 받다 → make a ＿＿＿＿＿＿＿＿

3 면접에 낙제하다 → ＿＿＿＿＿＿＿＿ the interview

4 시험에 합격하다 → ＿＿＿＿＿＿＿＿ the test

5 나의 수학 성적 → my math ＿＿＿＿＿＿＿s

6 쉬운 문제 → an ＿＿＿＿＿＿＿＿ problem

7 어려운 과제 → a ＿＿＿＿＿＿＿＿ task

8 보고서를 끝내다 → ＿＿＿＿＿＿＿＿ the report

9 시험에서 부정행위 하다 → ＿＿＿＿＿＿＿＿ on an exam

10 시험을 치르다 → take an ＿＿＿＿＿＿＿＿

| 보기 | | | | |
|---|---|---|---|---|
| homework | review | example | study | advice |
| effort | group | problem | excuse | explain |

## A 우리말 뜻을 보고 알맞은 단어를 보기 에서 찾아 쓰세요.

1 숙제 → _____  2 공부하다 → _____

3 문제 → _____  4 복습하다 → _____

5 그룹, 모임 → _____  6 예, 본보기 → _____

7 노력 → _____  8 변명 → _____

9 충고 → _____  10 설명하다 → _____

## B 우리말을 보고 보기 에서 알맞은 단어를 찾아 영어표현을 완성하세요.

1 그룹으로 작업하다 → work in _____ s

2 시험 공부하다 → _____ for an exam

3 숙제를 하다 → do my _____

4 교과서를 복습하다 → _____ the textbook

5 문제를 풀다 → solve a _____

6 예를 들다 → give an _____

7 노력하다 → make an _____

8 충고 하나 → a piece of _____

9 변명하다 → make an _____

10 설명하기 어려운 → difficult to _____

| 보기 | stationery | stapler | chalk | sketchbook | album |
|---|---|---|---|---|---|
| | clipboard | compass | folder | highlighter | scissors |

**A** 우리말 뜻을 보고 알맞은 단어를 보기 에서 찾아 쓰세요.

1 앨범 →

2 폴더 →

3 분필 →

4 가위 →

5 스테이플러 →

6 스케치북 →

7 나침반 →

8 클립보드 →

9 형광펜 →

10 문구류 →

**B** 우리말을 보고 보기 에서 알맞은 단어를 찾아 영어표현을 완성하세요.

1 우표 앨범 → a stamp _____

2 분필 한 개 → a piece of _____

3 폴더에 → in a _____

4 내 스테이플러 → my own _____

5 내 스케치북에 → in my _____

6 가위 한 자루 → a pair of _____

7 새 클립보드 → a new _____

8 지도와 나침반 → a map and _____

9 문구점 → a _____ store

10 형광펜으로 → with a _____

| 보기 | vacation | wonderful | country | wait | during |
|---|---|---|---|---|---|
| | forget | remember | planner | participate | leisure |

## A 우리말 뜻을 보고 알맞은 단어를 보기 에서 찾아 쓰세요.

1 잊다 → _____   2 기다리다 → _____

3 기억하다 → _____   4 방학 → _____

5 계획표 → _____   6 여가 → _____

7 ~ 동안 → _____   8 시골 → _____

9 아주 멋진 → _____   10 참여하다 → _____

## B 우리말을 보고 보기 에서 알맞은 단어를 찾아 영어표현을 완성하세요.

1 봄을 기다리다 → _____ for spring

2 답장하는 것을 잊다 → _____ to write back

3 여름방학 → the summer _____

4 겨울 동안 → _____ the winter

5 방학 계획표 → a vacation _____

6 아주 멋진 시간 → a _____ time

7 시골에서 살다 → live in the _____

8 그것을 확실히 기억하다 → _____ it clearly

9 내 여가 활동 → my _____ activity

10 활동에 참여하다 → _____ in an activity

| 보기 | picnic | basket | contest | happen | hurry |
|---|---|---|---|---|---|
| | leave | pick | special | activity | volunteer |

**A** 우리말 뜻을 보고 알맞은 단어를 보기 에서 찾아 쓰세요.

1 (꽃을) 꺾다 → 

2 소풍 → 

3 바구니 → 

4 떠나다 → 

5 서두르다 → 

6 대회 → 

7 활동 → 

8 특별한 → 

9 일어나다 → 

10 지원자 → 

**B** 우리말을 보고 보기 에서 알맞은 단어를 찾아 영어표현을 완성하세요.

1 소풍을 가다 → go on a _____

2 꽃을 꺾다 → _____ flowers

3 서둘러 가다 → _____ up and go

4 곧 떠나다 → _____ soon

5 소풍 바구니 → a picnic _____

6 장기자랑 대회 → a talent _____

7 특별한 친구 → a _____ friend

8 나에게 일어나다 → _____ to me

9 야외활동 → an outdoor _____

10 지원자가 필요하다 → need a _____

| 보기 | | | | | |
|---|---|---|---|---|---|
| march | field | playground | match | winner | |
| cheer | medal | block | loser | whistle | |

**A** 우리말 뜻을 보고 알맞은 단어를 보기 에서 찾아 쓰세요.

1 메달 → _____    2 경기, 시합 → _____

3 경기장 → _____    4 운동장 → _____

5 승자 → _____    6 패자 → _____

7 막다 → _____    8 호루라기 → _____

9 행진하다 → _____    10 응원하다 → _____

**B** 우리말을 보고 보기 에서 알맞은 단어를 찾아 영어표현을 완성하세요.

1 큰 경기 → a big _____

2 금메달을 따다 → win a gold _____

3 학교 운동장 → a school _____

4 운동 경기장 → a sports _____

5 슛을 막다 → _____ a shot

6 깨끗이 승복하는 패자 → a good _____

7 게임의 승자 → the _____ of a game

8 시청까지 행진하다 → _____ to City Hall

9 우리 선수들을 응원하다 → _____ for our players

10 호루라기를 불다 → blow a _____

| 보기 | enter | congratulation | memory | graduate | proud |
|---|---|---|---|---|---|
| | beginning | honor | kindergarten | elementary | university |

## A 우리말 뜻을 보고 알맞은 단어를 보기 에서 찾아 쓰세요.

1 유치원 →

2 대학 →

3 자랑스러운 →

4 우등, 명예 →

5 기억 →

6 초반, 시작 →

7 축하 →

8 초등의 →

9 졸업하다 →

10 입학하다 →

## B 우리말을 보고 보기 에서 알맞은 단어를 찾아 영어표현을 완성하세요.

1 학교에 입학하다 → _____ a school

2 하버드를 졸업하다 → _____ from Harvard

3 내 자신이 자랑스러운 → _____ of myself

4 선명한 기억 → a clear _____

5 우등상을 타다 → win an _____ prize

6 처음에는 → in the _____

7 축하 편지 → a letter of _____

8 대학 교수 → a _____ professor

9 초등학생들 → _____ students

10 유치원에 다니다 → go to _____

| 보기 | | | | |
|---|---|---|---|---|
| cleanup | messy | dusty | post | wipe |
| empty | repair | restroom | polish | tidy |

**A** 우리말 뜻을 보고 알맞은 단어를 보기 에서 찾아 쓰세요.

1 닦다 →

2 붙이다 →

3 비우다, 빈 →

4 고치다 →

5 깨끗한 →

6 지저분한 →

7 먼지투성이인 →

8 광을 내다 →

9 청소 →

10 (공공)화장실 →

**B** 우리말을 보고 보기 에서 알맞은 단어를 찾아 영어표현을 완성하세요.

1 깨끗한 부엌 → a _____ kitchen

2 지저분한 방 → a _____ room

3 먼지투성이 길 → a _____ road

4 창문을 닦다 → _____ off the window

5 문을 고치다 → _____ a door

6 사진을 붙이다 → _____ photos

7 내 신발에 광을 내다 → _____ my shoes

8 쓰레기통을 비우다 → _____ a trash can

9 화장실을 청소하다 → clean a _____

10 청소 캠페인 → a _____ campaign

| 보기 | concert | classical | entertain | popular | poor |
|---|---|---|---|---|---|
| | good | perform | express | imagine | audience |

**A** 우리말 뜻을 보고 알맞은 단어를 보기 에서 찾아 쓰세요.

1 잘하는 → _____

2 못하는 → _____

3 콘서트 → _____

4 클래식의 → _____

5 관객 → _____

6 상상하다 → _____

7 표현하다 → _____

8 공연하다 → _____

9 인기 있는 → _____

10 즐겁게 하다 → _____

**B** 우리말을 보고 보기 에서 알맞은 단어를 찾아 영어표현을 완성하세요.

1 콘서트를 열다 → give a _____

2 노래를 못하는 → _____ at singing

3 운동을 잘하는 → _____ at sports

4 세상을 상상하다 → _____ a world

5 내 자신을 표현하다 → _____ myself

6 아이들을 즐겁게 하다 → _____ children

7 클래식 음악 → _____ music

8 연극을 공연하다 → _____ a play

9 모두에게 인기 있는 → _____ with everyone

10 많은 관객 → a large _____

| 보기 | idea | decorate | bow | traditional | respect |
|---|---|---|---|---|---|
| | holiday | merry | touching | impressive | terrific |

**A** 우리말 뜻을 보고 알맞은 단어를 보기 에서 찾아 쓰세요.

1 절하다 → _____  2 방안, 생각 → _____

3 즐거운 → _____  4 휴일 → _____

5 장식하다 → _____  6 아주 멋진 → _____

7 감동적인 → _____  8 존경하다 → _____

9 전통적인 → _____  10 인상적인 → _____

**B** 우리말을 보고 보기 에서 알맞은 단어를 찾아 영어표현을 완성하세요.

1 국경일(국가의 휴일) → a national _____

2 좋은 방안이 있다 → have a good _____

3 조부모님께 절하다 → _____ to my grandparents

4 부모님을 존경하다 → _____ my parents

5 방을 장식하다 → _____ a room

6 즐거운 크리스마스 → a _____ Christmas

7 아주 멋져 보이다 → look _____

8 감동적인 이야기 → a _____ story

9 전통 한국 무용 → _____ Korean dance

10 인상적인 장소 → an _____ place

| 보기 | | | | |
|---|---|---|---|---|
| job | hire | task | business | company |
| office | pilot | artist | soldier | counselor |

## A 우리말 뜻을 보고 알맞은 단어를 보기 에서 찾아 쓰세요.

1 일, 직무 → _____  2 직업, 직장 → _____

3 조종사 → _____  4 고용하다 → _____

5 군인 → _____  6 회사 → _____

7 상담사 → _____  8 사무실 → _____

9 사업(체) → _____  10 예술가, 아티스트 → _____

## B 우리말을 보고 보기 에서 알맞은 단어를 찾아 영어표현을 완성하세요.

1 직장을 구하다 → get a _____

2 일을 하다 → do a _____

3 외국인 노동자를 고용하다 → _____ foreign workers

4 비행기 조종사 → an airline _____

5 그래픽 아티스트 → a graphic _____

6 사무실을 열다 → open an _____

7 컴퓨터 회사 → a computer _____

8 사업체를 운영하다 → run a _____

9 군인이 되다 → become a _____

10 상담을 받다(상담사를 보다) → see a _____

| 보기 | | | | |
|---|---|---|---|---|
| place | town | village | located | hotel |
| bakery | library | bookstore | airport | station |

**A** 우리말 뜻을 보고 알맞은 단어를 보기 에서 찾아 쓰세요.

1 (소)도시 →

2 마을 →

3 장소, 곳 →

4 호텔 →

5 서점 →

6 역 →

7 공항 →

8 제과점 →

9 도서관 →

10 ~에 위치한 →

**B** 우리말을 보고 보기 에서 알맞은 단어를 찾아 영어표현을 완성하세요.

1 호텔에 머물다 → stay in a _____

2 제과점을 운영하다 → run a _____

3 도서관을 이용하다 → use a _____

4 온라인 서점 → an online _____

5 공항에 도착하다 → arrive at the _____

6 지하철역 → a subway _____

7 가장 가까운 (소)도시 → the nearest _____

8 어촌(고기 잡는 마을) → a fishing _____

9 방문할 곳 → a _____ to visit

10 파리에 위치한 → _____ in Paris

| 보기 | nation | capital | abroad | building | crowded |
|---|---|---|---|---|---|
| | busy | metropolis | outskirt | facility | local |

## A  우리말 뜻을 보고 알맞은 단어를 보기 에서 찾아 쓰세요.

1  복잡한, 바쁜  →  _____      2  국가  →  _____

3  건물  →  _____      4  수도  →  _____

5  해외에  →  _____      6  시설  →  _____

7  붐비는  →  _____      8  대도시  →  _____

9  지역 [현지]의  →  _____      10  변두리, 교외  →  _____

## B  우리말을 보고 보기 에서 알맞은 단어를 찾아 영어표현을 완성하세요.

1  아시아 국가들  →  Asian _____ s

2  해외에 가다  →  go _____

3  고층 건물  →  a tall _____

4  복잡한 도로  →  a _____ road

5  지역 학교  →  a _____ school

6  한국의 수도  →  the _____ of Korea

7  엄청 붐비다  →  be so _____

8  의료 시설  →  a medical _____

9  런던의 변두리  →  the _____ of London

10  현대적 대도시  →  a modern _____

| 보기 | | | | |
|---|---|---|---|---|
| world | global | peace | war | island |
| continent | polar | human | iceberg | erupt |

## A 우리말 뜻을 보고 알맞은 단어를 보기 에서 찾아 쓰세요.

1 섬 → _____ 2 지구의 → _____

3 전쟁 → _____ 4 평화 → _____

5 인간[인류]의 → _____ 6 빙산 → _____

7 대륙 → _____ 8 분출하다 → _____

9 세계, 세상 → _____ 10 북극[남극]의 → _____

## B 우리말을 보고 보기 에서 알맞은 단어를 찾아 영어표현을 완성하세요.

1 북극곰 → a _____ bear

2 세상에서 → in the _____

3 전쟁 중에 → during the _____

4 평화롭게 → in _____

5 화산에서 분출하다 → _____ from a volcano

6 섬나라 → an _____ country

7 지구 온난화 → _____ warming

8 인류역사에서 → in _____ history

9 아프리카 대륙 → the African _____

10 빙산에 부딪치다 → hit an _____

| 보기 | marry | date | single | couple | wedding |
| --- | --- | --- | --- | --- | --- |
| | divorce | propose | bride | groom | honeymoon |

## A 우리말 뜻을 보고 알맞은 단어를 보기 에서 찾아 쓰세요.

1　데이트　→ _____

2　신부　→ _____

3　신랑　→ _____

4　이혼　→ _____

5　결혼식　→ _____

6　결혼하다　→ _____

7　청혼하다　→ _____

8　신혼여행　→ _____

9　부부, 한 쌍　→ _____

10　미혼 [혼자]의 → _____

## B 우리말을 보고 보기 에서 알맞은 단어를 찾아 영어표현을 완성하세요.

1　미혼이다　→ be _____

2　그녀와 결혼하다　→ _____ her

3　데이트가 있다　→ have a _____

4　새 신부　→ a new _____

5　신랑의 친구들　→ friends of the _____

6　젊은 부부　→ a young _____

7　이혼하다　→ get a _____

8　결혼식에 참석하다　→ attend a _____

9　그녀에게 청혼하다　→ _____ to her

10　그들의 신혼여행으로　→ on their _____

| 보기 | | | | |
|---|---|---|---|---|
| environment | issue | plastic | paper | dump |
| protect | recycle | destroy | harm | pollution |

## A 우리말 뜻을 보고 알맞은 단어를 보기 에서 찾아 쓰세요.

1  종이  →

2  버리다  →

3  해, 해악  →

4  보호하다  →

5  파괴하다  →

6  재활용하다  →

7  오염  →

8  환경  →

9  쟁점, 문제  →

10  플라스틱 [비닐](의)  →

## B 우리말을 보고 보기 에서 알맞은 단어를 찾아 영어표현을 완성하세요.

1  해를 끼치다  →  do _____

2  핵심 쟁점  →  a key _____

3  비닐봉지  →  a _____ bag

4  종이 한 장  →  a piece of _____

5  폐기물을 버리다  →  _____ waste

6  병을 재활용하다  →  _____ bottles

7  자연을 보호하다  →  _____ nature

8  대기 오염  →  air _____

9  도시를 파괴하다  →  _____ a city

10  환경에 나쁜  →  bad for the _____

| 보기 | accident | result | terrible | lucky | flood |
|------|----------|--------|----------|-------|-------|
| | earthquake | fall | cause | crash | suffer |

## A 우리말 뜻을 보고 알맞은 단어를 보기 에서 찾아 쓰세요.

1 결과 → _____

2 홍수, 범람 → _____

3 사고 → _____

4 지진 → _____

5 끔찍한 → _____

6 운이 좋은 → _____

7 충돌하다 → _____

8 고생하다 → _____

9 떨어지다 → _____

10 일으키다 → _____

## B 우리말을 보고 보기 에서 알맞은 단어를 찾아 영어표현을 완성하세요.

1 계단에서 떨어지다 → _____ down stairs

2 나무에 충돌하다 → _____ into a tree

3 알레르기로 고생하다 → _____ from allergies

4 홍수를 일으키다 → _____ flooding

5 범람하다 → be in _____

6 운 좋게 살아남다 → be _____ to survive

7 끔찍한 소식 → _____ news

8 결과적으로 → as a _____

9 사고를 당하다 → have an _____

10 강력한 지진 → a powerful _____

보기

| | | | | |
|---|---|---|---|---|
| pray | temple | god | sin | forgive |
| believe | life | death | sin | religion |
| | | | create | |

## A 우리말 뜻을 보고 알맞은 단어를 보기 에서 찾아 쓰세요.

1 신 → _____ 2 죽음 → _____

3 종교 → _____ 4 죄, 죄악 → _____

5 삶, 생명 → _____ 6 믿다 → _____

7 사원, 절 → _____ 8 창조하다 → _____

9 용서하다 → _____ 10 기도[기원]하다 → _____

## B 우리말을 보고 보기 에서 알맞은 단어를 찾아 영어표현을 완성하세요.

1 그리스 신들 → Greek _____ s

2 평화를 기원하다 → _____ for peace

3 죄를 짓다 → commit a _____

4 하느님을 믿다 → _____ in God

5 그녀의 생명을 구하다 → save her _____

6 절에 다니다 → go to _____

7 세상을 창조하다 → _____ the world

8 죽음을 면하다 → escape _____

9 용서하고 잊다 → _____ and forget

10 다른 종교들 → different _____ s

| 보기 | animal | species | raise | live | kingdom |
|---|---|---|---|---|---|
| | wild | domestic | feed | beast | prey |

## A 우리말 뜻을 보고 알맞은 단어를 보기 에서 찾아 쓰세요.

1 동물 →

2 먹이[사냥감] →

3 짐승 →

4 종류, (생물) 종 →

5 살다 →

6 야생(의) →

7 왕국 →

8 먹이를 주다 →

9 기르다, 재배하다 →

10 (동물이) 사육되는 →

## B 우리말을 보고 보기 에서 알맞은 단어를 찾아 영어표현을 완성하세요.

1 쉬운 먹이 → easy _____

2 닭을 기르다 → _____ chickens

3 야생 동물들 → wild _____ s

4 개에게 먹이를 주다 → _____ a dog

5 동굴에서 살다 → _____ in a cave

6 동물의 왕국 → the animal _____

7 멸종 위기 종 → endangered _____

8 야생에서 → in the _____

9 새도 짐승도 아닌 → neither bird nor _____

10 가축(사육되는 동물들) → _____ animals

| 보기 | water | stem | thorn | root | bloom |
|---|---|---|---|---|---|
| | grow | dense | herb | native | vary |

**A** 우리말 뜻을 보고 알맞은 단어를 보기 에서 찾아 쓰세요.

1 줄기 →

2 자라다 →

3 뿌리 →

4 빽빽한 →

5 피다 →

6 허브 →

7 가시 →

8 물을 주다 →

9 다르다 →

10 토종의, 태어난 →

**B** 우리말을 보고 보기 에서 알맞은 단어를 찾아 영어표현을 완성하세요.

1 크게 자라다 → _____ tall

2 빽빽한 숲 → _____ forests

3 토종 식물들 → _____ plants

4 가시 없는 → without a _____

5 크기가 다르다 → _____ in size

6 허브에 대해 배우다 → learn about _____ s

7 굵은 줄기 → a thick _____

8 뿌리째 → by the _____ s

9 정원에 물을 주다 → _____ the garden

10 봄에 피다 → _____ in spring

| 보기 | insect | lay | spray | attack | caterpillar |
|------|--------|-----|-------|--------|-------------|
|      | hatch  | poison | spray helpful | harmful | pest |

보기: insect　lay　spray　attack　caterpillar
hatch　poison　helpful　harmful　pest

## A  우리말 뜻을 보고 알맞은 단어를 보기 에서 찾아 쓰세요.

1  낳다 →

2  곤충 →

3  이로운 →

4  부화하다 →

5  해로운 →

6  독 →

7  뿌리다 →

8  해충 →

9  공격하다 →

10  애벌레 →

## B  우리말을 보고 보기 에서 알맞은 단어를 찾아 영어표현을 완성하세요.

1  곤충을 채집하다 → collect _____s

2  병해충 → diseases and _____s

3  알을 낳다 → _____ an egg

4  이로운 곤충들 → _____ insects

5  치명적인 독 → a deadly _____

6  매우 해롭다 → be very _____

7  살충제를 뿌리다 → _____ pesticides

8  적을 공격하다 → _____ an enemy

9  초록 애벌레 → a green _____

10  막 부화하려 하다 → be about to _____

| 보기 | | | | |
|---|---|---|---|---|
| warm | clear | shower | forecast | cool |
| weather | sunshine | lightning | thunder | cloudy |

**A** 우리말 뜻을 보고 알맞은 단어를 보기 에서 찾아 쓰세요.

1 시원한 → _____   2 따뜻한 → _____

3 날씨 → _____   4 맑은 → _____

5 햇빛, 햇살 → _____   6 흐린 → _____

7 번개 → _____   8 예보 → _____

9 소나기 → _____   10 천둥 → _____


**B** 우리말을 보고 보기 에서 알맞은 단어를 찾아 영어표현을 완성하세요.

1 겨울에 따뜻한 → _____ in winter

2 맑은 날에 → on _____ days

3 날씨를 예측하다 → predict the _____

4 봄 햇살 → the spring _____

5 갑작스런 소나기 → a sudden _____

6 일기 예보 → a weather _____

7 천둥소리를 듣다 → hear the _____

8 약간 흐리다 → be a little _____

9 가을에 시원한 → _____ in autumn

10 번개처럼 → like _____

| 보기 | | | | | |
|---|---|---|---|---|---|
| street | speed | pedestrian | signal | traffic |
| way | bumper | crosswalk | parking | tow |

**A** 우리말 뜻을 보고 알맞은 단어를 보기 에서 찾아 쓰세요.

1 거리 → 　　　　　　　　2 교통 →

3 속도 → 　　　　　　　　4 길 →

5 보행자 → 　　　　　　　6 횡단보도 →

7 신호 → 　　　　　　　　8 주차 →

9 범퍼 → 　　　　　　　10 견인 →

**B** 우리말을 보고 보기 에서 알맞은 단어를 찾아 영어표현을 완성하세요.

1 부주의한 보행자 → a careless _____

2 정지 신호 → a stop _____

3 차가 꽉 찬(범퍼가 맞닿은) → _____ to bumper

4 교통 표지판 → a _____ sign

5 횡단보도로 건너다 → cross at the _____

6 거리에 → on the _____

7 전속력으로 → at full _____

8 주차장 → a _____ lot

9 견인차 → a _____ truck

10 길을 찾다 → find out the _____

| 보기 | fare | broken | underground | subway | driver |
|---|---|---|---|---|---|
| | transfer | highway | passenger | area | ticket |

**A** 우리말 뜻을 보고 알맞은 단어를 보기 에서 찾아 쓰세요.

1　지하의　→ _____

2　지하철　→ _____

3　고속도로　→ _____

4　운전사　→ _____

5　승객　→ _____

6　티켓, 표　→ _____

7　지역　→ _____

8　고장 난　→ _____

9　갈아타다　→ _____

10　요금　→ _____

**B** 우리말을 보고 보기 에서 알맞은 단어를 찾아 영어표현을 완성하세요.

1　지하철로　→ by _____

2　버스 요금　→ a bus _____

3　티켓을 사다　→ buy a _____

4　고장 난 엘리베이터　→ a _____ elevator

5　고속도로에서　→ on a _____

6　지하 주차장　→ an _____ parking lot

7　모든 승객들　→ all _____ s

8　택시 운전사　→ a taxi _____

9　기차로 갈아타다　→ _____ to a train

10　이 지역을 통과하다　→ go through this _____

| 보기 | | | | | |
|---|---|---|---|---|---|
| invent | energy | develop | charge | digital | |
| technology | machine | creative | switch | basic | |

## A 우리말 뜻을 보고 알맞은 단어를 보기 에서 찾아 쓰세요.

1　발명하다　→　_____

2　에너지　→　_____

3　(과학) 기술　→　_____

4　창의적인　→　_____

5　기계　→　_____

6　충전하다　→　_____

7　스위치　→　_____

8　디지털의　→　_____

9　기초의　→　_____

10　개발하다　→　_____

## B 우리말을 보고 보기 에서 알맞은 단어를 찾아 영어표현을 완성하세요.

1　풍력 에너지　→　wind _____

2　창의적 사고　→　_____ thinking

3　기초 과학　→　_____ science

4　신제품을 개발하다　→　_____ new products

5　전원 스위치　→　a power _____

6　스마트폰을 충전하다　→　_____ a smartphone

7　전화를 발명하다　→　_____ a telephone

8　첨단 기술　→　high _____

9　세탁기(세탁 기계)　→　a washing _____

10　디지털 카메라　→　a _____ camera

| 보기 | planet | valley | desert | forest | Pacific |
| --- | --- | --- | --- | --- | --- |
| | astronaut | space | spaceship | earth | ocean |

## A  우리말 뜻을 보고 알맞은 단어를 보기 에서 찾아 쓰세요.

1  지구    →                        2  우주    →

3  숲    →                        4  우주선    →

5  바다, 대양    →                        6  계곡    →

7  태평양    →                        8  사막    →

9  행성    →                        10  우주비행사    →

## B  우리말을 보고 보기 에서 알맞은 단어를 찾아 영어표현을 완성하세요.

1  우주선을 화성에 보내다    →    send a _____ to Mars

2  계곡으로 가다    →    go to _____ s

3  지구에    →    on the _____

4  숲에    →    in the _____

5  바다 경치    →    an _____ view

6  서태평양에    →    in the Western _____

7  우주비행사가 되다    →    become an _____

8  가장 작은 행성    →    the smallest _____

9  우주를 여행하다    →    travel in _____

10  사막에서 살아남다    →    survive in a _____

| 보기 | | | | |
|---|---|---|---|---|
| make | reserve | waiter | chef | restaurant |
| menu | order | medium | tip | well-done |

**A** 우리말 뜻을 보고 알맞은 단어를 보기 에서 찾아 쓰세요.

1  종업원 → _____  2  식당 → _____

3  요리사 → _____  4  메뉴 → _____

5  중간의 → _____  6  주문하다 → _____

7  팁을 주다 → _____  8  만들다 → _____

9  잘 익힌 → _____  10  예약하다 → _____

**B** 우리말을 보고 보기 에서 알맞은 단어를 찾아 영어표현을 완성하세요.

1  치킨을 주문하다 → _____ chicken

2  잘 익힌 스테이크 → a steak _____

3  우리를 위해 피자를 만들다 → _____ pizza for us

4  멋진 식당 → a nice _____

5  메뉴에서 → on the _____

6  자리를 예약하다 → _____ a table

7  수석 요리사 → a head _____

8  중간 온도 → a _____ heat

9  종업원들에게 팁을 주다 → _____ waiters

10  종업원으로 일하다 → work as a _____

| 보기 | post office | zip code | form | envelope | express |
| --- | --- | --- | --- | --- | --- |
| | airmail | postcard | package | direct | express regular |

**A** 우리말 뜻을 보고 알맞은 단어를 보기 에서 찾아 쓰세요.

1 소포 → _____

2 우체국 → _____

3 우편 번호 → _____

4 서식, 양식 → _____

5 직접적인 → _____

6 봉투 → _____

7 보통의 → _____

8 항공 우편 → _____

9 속달의 → _____

10 엽서 → _____

**B** 우리말을 보고 보기 에서 알맞은 단어를 찾아 영어표현을 완성하세요.

1 엽서를 받다 → get a _____

2 소포를 보내다 → send a _____

3 다이렉트(직접) 메일 → _____ mail

4 보통 우편 → _____ mail

5 항공 우편으로 → by _____

6 이 양식을 작성하다 → fill out this _____

7 속달 우편 → _____ mail

8 우편 번호를 입력하다 → enter a _____

9 우체국에서 → at a _____

10 봉투 안에 → in an _____

| | | | |
|---|---|---|---|
| fire station | police office | firefighter | policeman |
| save | fire | call | help | thief | steal |

**A** 우리말 뜻을 보고 알맞은 단어를 보기 에서 찾아 쓰세요.

1 도둑 → _____  2 소방서 → _____

3 훔치다 → _____  4 경찰서 → _____

5 구하다 → _____  6 불, 화재 → _____

7 소방관 → _____  8 전화 → _____

9 경찰관 → _____  10 도움 → _____

**B** 우리말을 보고 보기 에서 알맞은 단어를 찾아 영어표현을 완성하세요.

1 도둑을 잡다 → catch a _____

2 차를 훔치다 → _____ a car

3 자동차들에 불을 지르다 → set _____ to cars

4 숲을 구하다 → _____ the forest

5 전화를 받다 → get a _____

6 그의 도움으로 → with his _____

7 소방서에서 → at a _____

8 가장 가까운 경찰서 → the nearest _____

9 소방관이 되다 → become a _____

10 용감한 경찰관 → a brave _____

| 보기 | record | royal | guidebook | thing | outstanding |
|---|---|---|---|---|---|
| | museum | visitor | exhibition | palace | treasure |

## A 우리말 뜻을 보고 알맞은 단어를 보기 에서 찾아 쓰세요.

| | | | | | | |
|---|---|---|---|---|---|---|
| 1 | 보물 | → | | 2 | 박물관 | → |
| 3 | 방문객 | → | | 4 | 뛰어난 | → |
| 5 | 전시회 | → | | 6 | 궁전 | → |
| 7 | 기록 | → | | 8 | 안내서 | → |
| 9 | 왕(실)의 | → | | 10 | 물건 | → |

## B 우리말을 보고 보기 에서 알맞은 단어를 찾아 영어표현을 완성하세요.

1 놀라운 기록 → an amazing _____

2 옛 물건들을 전시하다 → display the old _____s

3 많은 방문객들 → many _____s

4 고궁(오래된 궁전) → an old _____

5 왕실의 피 → _____ blood

6 한국어 안내서 → a Korean_____

7 특별 전시회 → a special _____

8 박물관을 방문하다 → visit the _____

9 뛰어난 전시품 → an _____ exhibit

10 보물 지도 → a _____ map

| 보기 | | | | |
|---|---|---|---|---|
| flu | symptom | patient | pain | sick |
| clinic | shot | checkup | hospital | serious |

**A** 우리말 뜻을 보고 알맞은 단어를 보기 에서 찾아 쓰세요.

1 환자 → _____

2 병원 → _____

3 고통 → _____

4 심각한 → _____

5 진료소 → _____

6 독감 → _____

7 주사 → _____

8 증상 → _____

9 건강검진 → _____

10 아픈, 병든 → _____

**B** 우리말을 보고 보기 에서 알맞은 단어를 찾아 영어표현을 완성하세요.

1 병들다 → get _____

2 건강 진료소 → a health _____

3 많은 고통을 느끼다 → feel much _____

4 심각한 문제 → a _____ problem

5 독감에 걸리다 → catch the _____

6 환자들을 돌보다 → take care of _____s

7 흔한 증상 → a common _____

8 독감 주사를 맞다 → get a flu _____

9 특별한 건강검진 → a special _____

10 입원하다(병원에 머무르다) → stay in the _____

| 보기 | fantasy | mystery | trailer | interesting | theater |
|---|---|---|---|---|---|
| | horror | movie | action | preview | festival |

**A** 우리말 뜻을 보고 알맞은 단어를 보기 에서 찾아 쓰세요.

1 상상, 공상 → _____  2 극장 → _____

3 미스터리 → _____  4 영화 → _____

5 예고편 → _____  6 액션 → _____

7 재미있는 → _____  8 시사회 → _____

9 축제 → _____  10 공포 → _____

**B** 우리말을 보고 보기 에서 알맞은 단어를 찾아 영어표현을 완성하세요.

1 영화제(영화 축제) → a film _____

2 영화를 상영하다 → show a _____

3 기자 시사회 → a press _____

4 상상 세계에서 → in a _____ world

5 첫 번째 예고편 → the first _____

6 극장에 가다 → go to the _____

7 공포 영화 → a _____ film

8 액션 영화 → an _____ movie

9 재미있는 영화 → an _____ movie

10 미스터리로 가득 차다 → be filled with _____

| 보기 | elect | system | follow | politics | Congress |
|---|---|---|---|---|---|
| | freedom | equality | lead | impeach | agree |

## A 우리말 뜻을 보고 알맞은 단어를 보기 에서 찾아 쓰세요.

1 의회 [국회] → _____  2 선출하다 → _____

3 자유 → _____  4 동의하다 → _____

5 평등 → _____  6 제도, 체계 → _____

7 이끌다 → _____  8 따르다 → _____

9 탄핵하다 → _____  10 정치 → _____

## B 우리말을 보고 보기 에서 알맞은 단어를 찾아 영어표현을 완성하세요.

1 그 클럽을 이끌다 → _____ the club

2 의회에 출마하다 → run for _____

3 우리의 자유를 지키다 → keep our _____

4 인종 평등 → racial _____

5 대통령을 탄핵하다 → _____ the president

6 법률 제도 → legal _____

7 그 규칙을 따르다 → _____ the rule

8 그를 의장으로 선출하다 → _____ him chairman

9 협력하겠다고 동의하다 → _____ to cooperate

10 정치에 관심 있는 → interested in _____

| 보기 | | | | |
|---|---|---|---|---|
| crime | prison | situation | fact | law |
| lawyer | sentence | admit | judge | court |

**A** 우리말 뜻을 보고 알맞은 단어를 보기 에서 찾아 쓰세요.

| 1 | 선고 | → | | 2 | 범죄 | → | |
|---|---|---|---|---|---|---|---|
| 3 | 판사 | → | | 4 | 감옥 | → | |
| 5 | 상황 | → | | 6 | 변호사 | → | |
| 7 | 사실 | → | | 8 | 법 | → | |
| 9 | 법원, 법정 | → | | 10 | 인정하다 | → | |

**B** 우리말을 보고 보기 에서 알맞은 단어를 찾아 영어표현을 완성하세요.

1 폭력 범죄 → violent _____

2 감옥에서 → in _____

3 사실을 부인하다 → deny the _____

4 법원에 출두하다 → appear in _____

5 법을 지키다 → obey the _____

6 변호사를 선임하다 → hire a _____

7 선고를 내리다 → pass _____

8 진실을 인정하다 → _____ the truth

9 판사 앞에 → before a _____

10 혼란스러운 상황 → a confusing _____

보기

| money | exchange | recovery | economy | piggy bank |
| property | boom | account | news | tax |

**A** 우리말 뜻을 보고 알맞은 단어를 보기 에서 찾아 쓰세요.

1 계좌 →
2 돈 →
3 환전 →
4 돼지 저금통 →
5 소식, 뉴스 →
6 경제 →
7 세금 →
8 재산 →
9 회복 →
10 호황 →

**B** 우리말을 보고 보기 에서 알맞은 단어를 찾아 영어표현을 완성하세요.

1 약간의 돈을 저축하다 → save some _____

2 은행 계좌 → a bank _____

3 환율(환전 비율) → an _____ rate

4 담뱃세(담배 세금) → a _____ on cigarettes

5 경제 회복 → economic _____

6 호황을 누리다 → enjoy a _____

7 돼지 저금통에 → in a _____

8 기업 뉴스 → business _____

9 세계 경제 → the world _____

10 사유 재산 → private _____

| 보기 | | | | |
|---|---|---|---|---|
| before | to | past | into | behind |
| out of | after | above | below | in front of |

## A 우리말 뜻을 보고 알맞은 단어를 보기 에서 찾아 쓰세요.

1 위에 → 

2 전에 → 

3 아래에 → 

4 후에 → 

5 뒤에 → 

6 ~을 지나서 → 

7 앞에 → 

8 안으로 → 

9 ~로, ~을 향해 → 

10 밖으로 → 

## B 우리말을 보고 보기 에서 알맞은 단어를 찾아 영어표현을 완성하세요.

1 자기 전에 → _____ bed

2 구름 위에 → _____ the clouds

3 평균 아래에 → _____ average

4 거리로 → _____ the street

5 나를 지나치다 → walk _____ me

6 물속으로 → _____ the water

7 일이 끝난 후에 → _____ work

8 그 여성 뒤에 → _____ the woman

9 거울 앞에 → _____ the mirror

10 불타는 집 밖으로 → _____ the burning house

| | | | | |
|---|---|---|---|---|
| inside | more | senior | outside | top |
| bottom | accept | reject | less | junior |

**A** 우리말 뜻을 보고 알맞은 단어를 보기 에서 찾아 쓰세요.

1 맨 위 → _____   2 안(쪽)에 → _____

3 맨 아래 → _____   4 밖[바깥]에 → _____

5 받아들이다 → _____   6 더 적은 → _____

7 거절하다 → _____   8 후배 → _____

9 더 많은 → _____   10 선배 → _____

**B** 우리말을 보고 보기 에서 알맞은 단어를 찾아 영어표현을 완성하세요.

1 안에 들어오다 → come _____

2 밖에 나가다 → go _____

3 언덕 맨 위 → the _____ of the hill

4 맨 아래에 → at the _____

5 그 제안을 거절하다 → _____ the offer

6 더 많은 빵 → _____ bread

7 더 적은 시간 → _____ time

8 그의 후배들을 위해 → for his _____s

9 선배들을 따르다 → follow the _____s

10 그의 사과를 받아들이다 → _____ his apology

| 보기 | turn on | turn up | climb down | get on | turn off |
| | get off | turn down | put on | take off | climb up |

## A 우리말 뜻을 보고 알맞은 단어를 보기 에서 찾아 쓰세요.

1 내려오다 → _____

2 켜다 → _____

3 벗다 → _____

4 끄다 → _____

5 크게 하다 → _____

6 올라가다 → _____

7 약하게 하다 → _____

8 입다 → _____

9 (탈것을) 타다 → _____

10 (탈것에서) 내리다 → _____

## B 우리말을 보고 보기 에서 알맞은 단어를 찾아 영어표현을 완성하세요.

1 어디서 내려야 하는지 → where to _____

2 코트를 입다 → _____ a coat

3 신발을 벗다 → _____ shoes

4 불[전등]을 끄다 → _____ a light

5 버스에 타다 → _____ a bus

6 선풍기를 켜다 → _____ a fan

7 언덕을 오르다 → _____ a hill

8 나무에서 내려오다 → _____ a tree

9 불을 줄이다(약하게 하다) → _____ the heat

10 볼륨을 크게 하다 → _____ the volume

# ANSWERS 정답

## Unit 01

A
| 1 | classmate | 2 | teach |
|---|---|---|---|
| 3 | present | 4 | absent |
| 5 | principal | 6 | pupil |
| 7 | semester | 8 | schedule |
| 9 | education | 10 | cafeteria |

B
| 1 | teach | 2 | pupils |
|---|---|---|---|
| 3 | absent | 4 | semester |
| 5 | present | 6 | schedule |
| 7 | principal | 8 | classmate |
| 9 | cafeteria | 10 | education |

## Unit 02

A
| 1 | music | 2 | art |
|---|---|---|---|
| 3 | history | 4 | science |
| 5 | subject | 6 | lesson |
| 7 | learn | 8 | understand |
| 9 | tutor | 10 | curriculum |

B
| 1 | art | 2 | history |
|---|---|---|---|
| 3 | music | 4 | science |
| 5 | subject | 6 | tutor |
| 7 | lessons | 8 | learn |
| 9 | understand | 10 | curriculum |

## Unit 03

A
| 1 | easy | 2 | answer |
|---|---|---|---|
| 3 | score | 4 | pass |
| 5 | fail | 6 | grade |
| 7 | difficult | 8 | finish |
| 9 | examination | 10 | cheat |

B
| 1 | answer | 2 | score |
|---|---|---|---|
| 3 | fail | 4 | pass |
| 5 | grades | 6 | easy |
| 7 | difficult | 8 | finish |
| 9 | cheat | 10 | examination |

## Unit 04

A
| 1 | homework | 2 | study |
|---|---|---|---|
| 3 | problem | 4 | review |
| 5 | group | 6 | example |
| 7 | effort | 8 | excuse |
| 9 | advice | 10 | explain |

B
| 1 | groups | 2 | study |
|---|---|---|---|
| 3 | homework | 4 | review |
| 5 | problem | 6 | example |
| 7 | effort | 8 | advice |
| 9 | excuse | 10 | explain |

## Unit 05

A
| 1 | album | 2 | folder |
|---|---|---|---|
| 3 | chalk | 4 | scissors |
| 5 | stapler | 6 | sketchbook |
| 7 | compass | 8 | clipboard |
| 9 | highlighter | 10 | stationery |

B
| 1 | album | 2 | chalk |
|---|---|---|---|
| 3 | folder | 4 | stapler |
| 5 | sketchbook | 6 | scissors |
| 7 | clipboard | 8 | compass |
| 9 | stationery | 10 | highlighter |

## Unit 06

A
| 1 | forget | 2 | wait |
|---|---|---|---|
| 3 | remember | 4 | vacation |
| 5 | planner | 6 | leisure |
| 7 | during | 8 | country |
| 9 | wonderful | 10 | participate |

B
| 1 | wait | 2 | forget |
|---|---|---|---|
| 3 | vacation | 4 | during |
| 5 | planner | 6 | wonderful |
| 7 | country | 8 | remember |
| 9 | leisure | 10 | participate |

## Unit 07

**A**
| | | | |
|---|---|---|---|
| 1 | pick | 2 | picnic |
| 3 | basket | 4 | leave |
| 5 | hurry | 6 | contest |
| 7 | activity | 8 | special |
| 9 | happen | 10 | volunteer |

**B**
| | | | |
|---|---|---|---|
| 1 | picnic | 2 | pick |
| 3 | hurry | 4 | leave |
| 5 | basket | 6 | contest |
| 7 | special | 8 | happen |
| 9 | activity | 10 | volunteer |

## Unit 08

**A**
| | | | |
|---|---|---|---|
| 1 | medal | 2 | match |
| 3 | field | 4 | playground |
| 5 | winner | 6 | loser |
| 7 | block | 8 | whistle |
| 9 | march | 10 | cheer |

**B**
| | | | |
|---|---|---|---|
| 1 | match | 2 | medal |
| 3 | playground | 4 | field |
| 5 | block | 6 | loser |
| 7 | winner | 8 | march |
| 9 | cheer | 10 | whistle |

## Unit 09

**A**
| | | | |
|---|---|---|---|
| 1 | kindergarten | 2 | university |
| 3 | proud | 4 | honor |
| 5 | memory | 6 | beginning |
| 7 | congratulation | 8 | elementary |
| 9 | graduate | 10 | enter |

**B**
| | | | |
|---|---|---|---|
| 1 | enter | 2 | graduate |
| 3 | proud | 4 | memory |
| 5 | honor | 6 | beginning |
| 7 | congratulation | 8 | university |
| 9 | elementary | 10 | kindergarten |

## Unit 10

**A**
| | | | |
|---|---|---|---|
| 1 | wipe | 2 | post |
| 3 | empty | 4 | repair |
| 5 | tidy | 6 | messy |
| 7 | dusty | 8 | polish |
| 9 | cleanup | 10 | restroom |

**B**
| | | | |
|---|---|---|---|
| 1 | tidy | 2 | messy |
| 3 | dusty | 4 | wipe |
| 5 | repair | 6 | post |
| 7 | polish | 8 | empty |
| 9 | restroom | 10 | cleanup |

## Unit 11

**A**
| | | | |
|---|---|---|---|
| 1 | good | 2 | poor |
| 3 | concert | 4 | classical |
| 5 | audience | 6 | imagine |
| 7 | express | 8 | perform |
| 9 | popular | 10 | entertain |

**B**
| | | | |
|---|---|---|---|
| 1 | concert | 2 | poor |
| 3 | good | 4 | imagine |
| 5 | express | 6 | entertain |
| 7 | classical | 8 | perform |
| 9 | popular | 10 | audience |

## Unit 12

**A**
| | | | |
|---|---|---|---|
| 1 | bow | 2 | idea |
| 3 | merry | 4 | holiday |
| 5 | decorate | 6 | terrific |
| 7 | touching | 8 | respect |
| 9 | traditional | 10 | impressive |

**B**
| | | | |
|---|---|---|---|
| 1 | holiday | 2 | idea |
| 3 | bow | 4 | respect |
| 5 | decorate | 6 | merry |
| 7 | terrific | 8 | touching |
| 9 | traditional | 10 | impressive |

## Unit 13

**A**
| 1 | task | 2 | job |
|---|------|---|-----|
| 3 | pilot | 4 | hire |
| 5 | soldier | 6 | company |
| 7 | counselor | 8 | office |
| 9 | business | 10 | artist |

**B**
| 1 | job | 2 | task |
|---|-----|---|------|
| 3 | hire | 4 | pilot |
| 5 | artist | 6 | office |
| 7 | company | 8 | business |
| 9 | soldier | 10 | counselor |

## Unit 14

**A**
| 1 | town | 2 | village |
|---|------|---|---------|
| 3 | place | 4 | hotel |
| 5 | bookstore | 6 | station |
| 7 | airport | 8 | bakery |
| 9 | library | 10 | located |

**B**
| 1 | hotel | 2 | bakery |
|---|-------|---|--------|
| 3 | library | 4 | bookstore |
| 5 | airport | 6 | station |
| 7 | town | 8 | village |
| 9 | place | 10 | located |

## Unit 15

**A**
| 1 | busy | 2 | nation |
|---|------|---|--------|
| 3 | building | 4 | capital |
| 5 | abroad | 6 | facility |
| 7 | crowded | 8 | metropolis |
| 9 | local | 10 | outskirt |

**B**
| 1 | nations | 2 | abroad |
|---|---------|---|--------|
| 3 | building | 4 | busy |
| 5 | local | 6 | capital |
| 7 | crowded | 8 | facility |
| 9 | outskirt | 10 | metropolis |

## Unit 16

**A**
| 1 | island | 2 | global |
|---|--------|---|--------|
| 3 | war | 4 | peace |
| 5 | human | 6 | iceberg |
| 7 | continent | 8 | erupt |
| 9 | world | 10 | polar |

**B**
| 1 | polar | 2 | world |
|---|-------|---|-------|
| 3 | war | 4 | peace |
| 5 | erupt | 6 | island |
| 7 | global | 8 | human |
| 9 | continent | 10 | iceberg |

## Unit 17

**A**
| 1 | date | 2 | bride |
|---|------|---|-------|
| 3 | groom | 4 | divorce |
| 5 | wedding | 6 | marry |
| 7 | propose | 8 | honeymoon |
| 9 | couple | 10 | single |

**B**
| 1 | single | 2 | marry |
|---|--------|---|-------|
| 3 | date | 4 | bride |
| 5 | groom | 6 | couple |
| 7 | divorce | 8 | wedding |
| 9 | propose | 10 | honeymoon |

## Unit 18

**A**
| 1 | paper | 2 | dump |
|---|-------|---|------|
| 3 | harm | 4 | protect |
| 5 | destroy | 6 | recycle |
| 7 | pollution | 8 | environment |
| 9 | issue | 10 | plastic |

**B**
| 1 | harm | 2 | issue |
|---|------|---|-------|
| 3 | plastic | 4 | paper |
| 5 | dump | 6 | recycle |
| 7 | protect | 8 | pollution |
| 9 | destroy | 10 | environment |

## Unit 19

**A**
| | | | |
|---|---|---|---|
| 1 | result | 2 | flood |
| 3 | accident | 4 | earthquake |
| 5 | terrible | 6 | lucky |
| 7 | crash | 8 | suffer |
| 9 | fall | 10 | cause |

**B**
| | | | |
|---|---|---|---|
| 1 | fall | 2 | crash |
| 3 | suffer | 4 | cause |
| 5 | flood | 6 | lucky |
| 7 | terrible | 8 | result |
| 9 | accident | 10 | earthquake |

## Unit 20

**A**
| | | | |
|---|---|---|---|
| 1 | god | 2 | death |
| 3 | religion | 4 | sin |
| 5 | life | 6 | believe |
| 7 | temple | 8 | create |
| 9 | forgive | 10 | pray |

**B**
| | | | |
|---|---|---|---|
| 1 | gods | 2 | pray |
| 3 | sin | 4 | believe |
| 5 | life | 6 | temple |
| 7 | create | 8 | death |
| 9 | forgive | 10 | religions |

## Unit 21

**A**
| | | | |
|---|---|---|---|
| 1 | animal | 2 | prey |
| 3 | beast | 4 | species |
| 5 | live | 6 | wild |
| 7 | kingdom | 8 | feed |
| 9 | raise | 10 | domestic |

**B**
| | | | |
|---|---|---|---|
| 1 | prey | 2 | raise |
| 3 | animals | 4 | feed |
| 5 | live | 6 | kingdom |
| 7 | species | 8 | wild |
| 9 | beast | 10 | domestic |

## Unit 22

**A**
| | | | |
|---|---|---|---|
| 1 | stem | 2 | grow |
| 3 | root | 4 | dense |
| 5 | bloom | 6 | herb |
| 7 | thorn | 8 | water |
| 9 | vary | 10 | native |

**B**
| | | | |
|---|---|---|---|
| 1 | grow | 2 | dense |
| 3 | native | 4 | thorn |
| 5 | vary | 6 | herbs |
| 7 | stem | 8 | roots |
| 9 | water | 10 | bloom |

## Unit 23

**A**
| | | | |
|---|---|---|---|
| 1 | lay | 2 | insect |
| 3 | helpful | 4 | hatch |
| 5 | harmful | 6 | poison |
| 7 | spray | 8 | pest |
| 9 | attack | 10 | caterpillar |

**B**
| | | | |
|---|---|---|---|
| 1 | insects | 2 | pests |
| 3 | lay | 4 | helpful |
| 5 | poison | 6 | harmful |
| 7 | spray | 8 | attack |
| 9 | caterpillar | 10 | hatch |

## Unit 24

**A**
| | | | |
|---|---|---|---|
| 1 | cool | 2 | warm |
| 3 | weather | 4 | clear |
| 5 | sunshine | 6 | cloudy |
| 7 | lightning | 8 | forecast |
| 9 | shower | 10 | thunder |

**B**
| | | | |
|---|---|---|---|
| 1 | warm | 2 | clear |
| 3 | weather | 4 | sunshine |
| 5 | shower | 6 | forecast |
| 7 | thunder | 8 | cloudy |
| 9 | cool | 10 | lightning |

## Unit 25

| A | | | |
|---|---|---|---|
| 1 | street | 2 | traffic |
| 3 | speed | 4 | way |
| 5 | pedestrian | 6 | crosswalk |
| 7 | signal | 8 | parking |
| 9 | bumper | 10 | tow |

| B | | | |
|---|---|---|---|
| 1 | pedestrian | 2 | signal |
| 3 | bumper | 4 | traffic |
| 5 | crosswalk | 6 | street |
| 7 | speed | 8 | parking |
| 9 | tow | 10 | way |

## Unit 26

| A | | | |
|---|---|---|---|
| 1 | underground | 2 | subway |
| 3 | highway | 4 | driver |
| 5 | passenger | 6 | ticket |
| 7 | area | 8 | broken |
| 9 | transfer | 10 | fare |

| B | | | |
|---|---|---|---|
| 1 | subway | 2 | fare |
| 3 | ticket | 4 | broken |
| 5 | highway | 6 | underground |
| 7 | passengers | 8 | driver |
| 9 | transfer | 10 | area |

## Unit 27

| A | | | |
|---|---|---|---|
| 1 | invent | 2 | energy |
| 3 | technology | 4 | creative |
| 5 | machine | 6 | charge |
| 7 | switch | 8 | digital |
| 9 | basic | 10 | develop |

| B | | | |
|---|---|---|---|
| 1 | energy | 2 | creative |
| 3 | basic | 4 | develop |
| 5 | switch | 6 | charge |
| 7 | invent | 8 | technology |
| 9 | machine | 10 | digital |

## Unit 28

| A | | | |
|---|---|---|---|
| 1 | earth | 2 | space |
| 3 | forest | 4 | spaceship |
| 5 | ocean | 6 | valley |
| 7 | Pacific | 8 | desert |
| 9 | planet | 10 | astronaut |

| B | | | |
|---|---|---|---|
| 1 | spaceship | 2 | valleys |
| 3 | earth | 4 | forest |
| 5 | ocean | 6 | Pacific |
| 7 | astronaut | 8 | planet |
| 9 | space | 10 | desert |

## Unit 29

| A | | | |
|---|---|---|---|
| 1 | waiter | 2 | restaurant |
| 3 | chef | 4 | menu |
| 5 | medium | 6 | order |
| 7 | tip | 8 | make |
| 9 | well-done | 10 | reserve |

| B | | | |
|---|---|---|---|
| 1 | order | 2 | well-done |
| 3 | make | 4 | restaurant |
| 5 | menu | 6 | reserve |
| 7 | chef | 8 | medium |
| 9 | tip | 10 | waiter |

## Unit 30

| A | | | |
|---|---|---|---|
| 1 | package | 2 | post office |
| 3 | zip code | 4 | form |
| 5 | direct | 6 | envelope |
| 7 | regular | 8 | airmail |
| 9 | express | 10 | postcard |

| B | | | |
|---|---|---|---|
| 1 | postcard | 2 | package |
| 3 | direct | 4 | regular |
| 5 | airmail | 6 | form |
| 7 | express | 8 | zip code |
| 9 | post office | 10 | envelope |

## Unit 31

**A**
1. thief
2. fire station
3. steal
4. police office
5. save
6. fire
7. firefighter
8. call
9. policeman
10. help

**B**
1. thief
2. steal
3. fire
4. save
5. call
6. help
7. fire station
8. police office
9. firefighter
10. policeman

## Unit 32

**A**
1. treasure
2. museum
3. visitor
4. outstanding
5. exhibition
6. palace
7. record
8. guidebook
9. royal
10. thing

**B**
1. record
2. things
3. visitors
4. palace
5. royal
6. guidebook
7. exhibition
8. museum
9. outstanding
10. treasure

## Unit 33

**A**
1. patient
2. hospital
3. pain
4. serious
5. clinic
6. flu
7. shot
8. symptom
9. checkup
10. sick

**B**
1. sick
2. clinic
3. pain
4. serious
5. flu
6. patients
7. symptom
8. shot
9. checkup
10. hospital

## Unit 34

**A**
1. fantasy
2. theater
3. mystery
4. movie
5. trailer
6. action
7. interesting
8. preview
9. festival
10. horror

**B**
1. festival
2. movie
3. preview
4. fantasy
5. trailer
6. theater
7. horror
8. action
9. interesting
10. mystery

## Unit 35

**A**
1. Congress
2. elect
3. freedom
4. agree
5. equality
6. system
7. lead
8. follow
9. impeach
10. politics

**B**
1. lead
2. Congress
3. freedom
4. equality
5. impeach
6. system
7. follow
8. elect
9. agree
10. politics

## Unit 36

**A**
1. sentence
2. crime
3. judge
4. prison
5. situation
6. lawyer
7. fact
8. law
9. court
10. admit

**B**
1. crime
2. prison
3. fact
4. court
5. law
6. lawyer
7. sentence
8. admit
9. judge
10. situation

## Unit 37

**A**
| | | | |
|---|---|---|---|
| 1 | account | 2 | money |
| 3 | exchange | 4 | piggy bank |
| 5 | news | 6 | economy |
| 7 | tax | 8 | property |
| 9 | recovery | 10 | boom |

**B**
| | | | |
|---|---|---|---|
| 1 | money | 2 | account |
| 3 | exchange | 4 | tax |
| 5 | recovery | 6 | boom |
| 7 | piggy bank | 8 | news |
| 9 | economy | 10 | property |

## Unit 38

**A**
| | | | |
|---|---|---|---|
| 1 | above | 2 | before |
| 3 | below | 4 | after |
| 5 | behind | 6 | past |
| 7 | in front of | 8 | into |
| 9 | to | 10 | out of |

**B**
| | | | |
|---|---|---|---|
| 1 | before | 2 | above |
| 3 | below | 4 | to |
| 5 | past | 6 | into |
| 7 | after | 8 | behind |
| 9 | in front of | 10 | out of |

## Unit 39

**A**
| | | | |
|---|---|---|---|
| 1 | top | 2 | inside |
| 3 | bottom | 4 | outside |
| 5 | accept | 6 | less |
| 7 | reject | 8 | junior |
| 9 | more | 10 | senior |

**B**
| | | | |
|---|---|---|---|
| 1 | inside | 2 | outside |
| 3 | top | 4 | bottom |
| 5 | reject | 6 | more |
| 7 | less | 8 | juniors |
| 9 | seniors | 10 | accept |

## Unit 40

**A**
| | | | |
|---|---|---|---|
| 1 | climb down | 2 | turn on |
| 3 | take off | 4 | turn off |
| 5 | turn up | 6 | climb up |
| 7 | turn down | 8 | put on |
| 9 | get on | 10 | get off |

**B**
| | | | |
|---|---|---|---|
| 1 | get off | 2 | put on |
| 3 | take off | 4 | turn off |
| 5 | get on | 6 | turn on |
| 7 | climb up | 8 | climb down |
| 9 | turn down | 10 | turn up |

Longman

# Longman

## Vocabulary MENTOR JOY

# 단어 쓰기 노트

# 3

Longman

# Vocabulary
## MENTOR
# JOY

# 단어 쓰기 노트

# 3

✎ 다음 단어의 우리말 뜻을 쓰고, 영어로 4번씩 반복해서 쓰세요.

| 1 | 2 | 3 | 4 | 5 |
|---|---|---|---|---|
| classmate | present | absent | teach | principal |
| 반 친구 | | | | |
| classmate | | | | |

| 6 | 7 | 8 | 9 | 10 |
|---|---|---|---|---|
| pupil | cafeteria | education | semester | schedule |
| | | | | |

✏️ 다음 단어의 우리말 뜻을 쓰고, 영어로 4번씩 반복해서 쓰세요.

| 1 | 2 | 3 | 4 | 5 |
|---|---|---|---|---|
| subject | science | music | history | art |
| 과목 | | | | |
| subject | | | | |

| 6 | 7 | 8 | 9 | 10 |
|---|---|---|---|---|
| learn | understand | lesson | curriculum | tutor |
| | | | | |

✎ 다음 단어의 우리말 뜻을 쓰고, 영어로 4번씩 반복해서 쓰세요.

| 1 | 2 | 3 | 4 | 5 |
|---|---|---|---|---|
| pass | fail | answer | examination | score |
| 합격하다 | | | | |
| pass | | | | |

| 6 | 7 | 8 | 9 | 10 |
|---|---|---|---|---|
| grade | easy | difficult | cheat | finish |
| | | | | |

✏️ 다음 단어의 우리말 뜻을 쓰고, 영어로 4번씩 반복해서 쓰세요.

| 1 | 2 | 3 | 4 | 5 |
| --- | --- | --- | --- | --- |
| homework | review | example | study | advice |
| 숙제 | | | | |
| homework | | | | |

| 6 | 7 | 8 | 9 | 10 |
| --- | --- | --- | --- | --- |
| effort | group | problem | excuse | explain |
| | | | | |

✎ 다음 단어의 우리말 뜻을 쓰고, 영어로 4번씩 반복해서 쓰세요.

| 1 | 2 | 3 | 4 | 5 |
|---|---|---|---|---|
| stationery | stapler | chalk | sketchbook | album |
| 문구류 | | | | |
| stationery | | | | |

| 6 | 7 | 8 | 9 | 10 |
|---|---|---|---|---|
| clipboard | compass | folder | highlighter | scissors |
| | | | | |

✏️ 다음 단어의 우리말 뜻을 쓰고, 영어로 4번씩 반복해서 쓰세요.

| 1 | 2 | 3 | 4 | 5 |
|---|---|---|---|---|
| vacation | wonderful | country | wait | during |
| 방학 | | | | |
| vacation | | | | |

| 6 | 7 | 8 | 9 | 10 |
|---|---|---|---|---|
| forget | remember | planner | participate | leisure |
| | | | | |

✎ 다음 단어의 우리말 뜻을 쓰고, 영어로 4번씩 반복해서 쓰세요.

| 1 | 2 | 3 | 4 | 5 |
|---|---|---|---|---|
| picnic | basket | contest | happen | hurry |
| 소풍 | | | | |
| picnic | | | | |

| 6 | 7 | 8 | 9 | 10 |
|---|---|---|---|---|
| leave | pick | special | activity | volunteer |
| | | | | |

다음 단어의 우리말 뜻을 쓰고, 영어로 4번씩 반복해서 쓰세요.

| 1 | 2 | 3 | 4 | 5 |
|---|---|---|---|---|
| march | field | playground | match | winner |
| 행진하다 | | | | |
| march | | | | |

| 6 | 7 | 8 | 9 | 10 |
|---|---|---|---|---|
| cheer | medal | block | loser | whistle |
| | | | | |

✎ 다음 단어의 우리말 뜻을 쓰고, 영어로 4번씩 반복해서 쓰세요.

| 1 | 2 | 3 | 4 | 5 |
|---|---|---|---|---|
| enter | congratulation | memory | graduate | proud |
| 입학하다 | | | | |
| enter | | | | |

| 6 | 7 | 8 | 9 | 10 |
|---|---|---|---|---|
| beginning | honor | kindergarten | elementary | university |
| | | | | |

✎ 다음 단어의 우리말 뜻을 쓰고, 영어로 4번씩 반복해서 쓰세요.

| 1 | 2 | 3 | 4 | 5 |
|---|---|---|---|---|
| cleanup | messy | dusty | tidy | post |
| 청소 | | | | |
| cleanup | | | | |

| 6 | 7 | 8 | 9 | 10 |
|---|---|---|---|---|
| wipe | empty | repair | polish | restroom |
| | | | | |

✎ 다음 단어의 우리말 뜻을 쓰고, 영어로 4번씩 반복해서 쓰세요.

| 1 | 2 | 3 | 4 | 5 |
| --- | --- | --- | --- | --- |
| concert | classical | popular | poor | good |
| 콘서트 | | | | |
| concert | | | | |

| 6 | 7 | 8 | 9 | 10 |
| --- | --- | --- | --- | --- |
| entertain | perform | express | imagine | audience |
| | | | | |

다음 단어의 우리말 뜻을 쓰고, 영어로 4번씩 반복해서 쓰세요.

| 1 | 2 | 3 | 4 | 5 |
|---|---|---|---|---|
| idea | decorate | bow | traditional | respect |
| 방안, 생각 | | | | |
| idea | | | | |

| 6 | 7 | 8 | 9 | 10 |
|---|---|---|---|---|
| holiday | merry | touching | impressive | terrific |
| | | | | |

다음 단어의 우리말 뜻을 쓰고, 영어로 4번씩 반복해서 쓰세요.

| 1 | 2 | 3 | 4 | 5 |
|---|---|---|---|---|
| job | hire | task | business | company |
| 직업, 직장 | | | | |
| job | | | | |

| 6 | 7 | 8 | 9 | 10 |
|---|---|---|---|---|
| office | pilot | artist | soldier | counselor |
| | | | | |

✎ 다음 단어의 우리말 뜻을 쓰고, 영어로 4번씩 반복해서 쓰세요.

| 1 | 2 | 3 | 4 | 5 |
|---|---|---|---|---|
| place | town | village | located | hotel |
| 장소, 곳 | | | | |
| place | | | | |

| 6 | 7 | 8 | 9 | 10 |
|---|---|---|---|---|
| bakery | library | bookstore | airport | station |
| | | | | |

✏️ 다음 단어의 우리말 뜻을 쓰고, 영어로 4번씩 반복해서 쓰세요.

| 1 | 2 | 3 | 4 | 5 |
|---|---|---|---|---|
| nation | capital | abroad | building | crowded |
| 국가 | | | | |
| nation | | | | |

| 6 | 7 | 8 | 9 | 10 |
|---|---|---|---|---|
| busy | metropolis | outskirt | facility | local |
| | | | | |

다음 단어의 우리말 뜻을 쓰고, 영어로 4번씩 반복해서 쓰세요.

| 1 | 2 | 3 | 4 | 5 |
|---|---|---|---|---|
| world | global | peace | war | island |
| 세계, 세상 | | | | |
| world | | | | |

| 6 | 7 | 8 | 9 | 10 |
|---|---|---|---|---|
| continent | polar | human | iceberg | erupt |

✎ 다음 단어의 우리말 뜻을 쓰고, 영어로 4번씩 반복해서 쓰세요.

| 1 | 2 | 3 | 4 | 5 |
|---|---|---|---|---|
| marry | date | single | couple | wedding |
| 결혼하다 | | | | |
| marry | | | | |

| 6 | 7 | 8 | 9 | 10 |
|---|---|---|---|---|
| divorce | propose | bride | groom | honeymoon |
| | | | | |

다음 단어의 우리말 뜻을 쓰고, 영어로 4번씩 반복해서 쓰세요.

| 1 | 2 | 3 | 4 | 5 |
|---|---|---|---|---|
| environment | issue | plastic | paper | dump |
| 환경 | | | | |
| environment | | | | |

| 6 | 7 | 8 | 9 | 10 |
|---|---|---|---|---|
| protect | recycle | destroy | harm | pollution |
| | | | | |

✏️ 다음 단어의 우리말 뜻을 쓰고, 영어로 4번씩 반복해서 쓰세요.

| 1 | 2 | 3 | 4 | 5 |
|---|---|---|---|---|
| accident | result | terrible | lucky | flood |
| 사고 | | | | |
| accident | | | | |

| 6 | 7 | 8 | 9 | 10 |
|---|---|---|---|---|
| earthquake | fall | cause | crash | suffer |
| | | | | |

✎ 다음 단어의 우리말 뜻을 쓰고, 영어로 4번씩 반복해서 쓰세요.

| 1 | 2 | 3 | 4 | 5 |
|---|---|---|---|---|
| pray | temple | god | sin | forgive |
| 기도[기원]하다 | | | | |
| pray | | | | |

| 6 | 7 | 8 | 9 | 10 |
|---|---|---|---|---|
| believe | life | death | create | religion |
| | | | | |

✏️ 다음 단어의 우리말 뜻을 쓰고, 영어로 4번씩 반복해서 쓰세요.

| 1 | 2 | 3 | 4 | 5 |
|---|---|---|---|---|
| animal | prey | raise | wild | domestic |
| 동물 | | | | |
| animal | | | | |

| 6 | 7 | 8 | 9 | 10 |
|---|---|---|---|---|
| feed | beast | live | kingdom | species |
| | | | | |

✎ 다음 단어의 우리말 뜻을 쓰고, 영어로 4번씩 반복해서 쓰세요.

| 1 | 2 | 3 | 4 | 5 |
|---|---|---|---|---|
| water | stem | root | bloom | grow |
| 물을 주다 | | | | |
| water | | | | |

| 6 | 7 | 8 | 9 | 10 |
|---|---|---|---|---|
| dense | herb | native | thorn | vary |
| | | | | |

✎ 다음 단어의 우리말 뜻을 쓰고, 영어로 4번씩 반복해서 쓰세요.

| 1 | 2 | 3 | 4 | 5 |
| --- | --- | --- | --- | --- |
| insect | lay | helpful | harmful | spray |
| 곤충 | | | | |
| insect | | | | |

| 6 | 7 | 8 | 9 | 10 |
| --- | --- | --- | --- | --- |
| attack | caterpillar | hatch | poison | pest |
| | | | | |

✎ 다음 단어의 우리말 뜻을 쓰고, 영어로 4번씩 반복해서 쓰세요.

| 1 | 2 | 3 | 4 | 5 |
|---|---|---|---|---|
| warm | clear | cloudy | cool | weather |
| 따뜻한 | | | | |
| warm | | | | |

| 6 | 7 | 8 | 9 | 10 |
|---|---|---|---|---|
| sunshine | lightning | shower | forecast | thunder |
| | | | | |

✎ 다음 단어의 우리말 뜻을 쓰고, 영어로 4번씩 반복해서 쓰세요.

| 1 | 2 | 3 | 4 | 5 |
|---|---|---|---|---|
| traffic | way | street | speed | pedestrian |
| 교통 | | | | |
| traffic | | | | |

| 6 | 7 | 8 | 9 | 10 |
|---|---|---|---|---|
| signal | bumper | crosswalk | parking | tow |
| | | | | |

다음 단어의 우리말 뜻을 쓰고, 영어로 4번씩 반복해서 쓰세요.

| 1 | 2 | 3 | 4 | 5 |
|---|---|---|---|---|
| subway | driver | transfer | fare | ticket |
| 지하철 | | | | |
| subway | | | | |

| 6 | 7 | 8 | 9 | 10 |
|---|---|---|---|---|
| broken | underground | highway | passenger | area |
| | | | | |

✎ 다음 단어의 우리말 뜻을 쓰고, 영어로 4번씩 반복해서 쓰세요.

| 1 | 2 | 3 | 4 | 5 |
|---|---|---|---|---|
| invent | technology | machine | energy | creative |
| 발명하다 | | | | |
| invent | | | | |

| 6 | 7 | 8 | 9 | 10 |
|---|---|---|---|---|
| charge | digital | develop | switch | basic |
| | | | | |

✎ 다음 단어의 우리말 뜻을 쓰고, 영어로 4번씩 반복해서 쓰세요.

| 1 | 2 | 3 | 4 | 5 |
|---|---|---|---|---|
| earth | forest | ocean | Pacific | valley |
| 지구 | | | | |
| earth | | | | |

| 6 | 7 | 8 | 9 | 10 |
|---|---|---|---|---|
| desert | space | spaceship | astronaut | planet |
| | | | | |

✏️ 다음 단어의 우리말 뜻을 쓰고, 영어로 4번씩 반복해서 쓰세요.

| 1 | 2 | 3 | 4 | 5 |
|---|---|---|---|---|
| restaurant | menu | order | make | reserve |
| 식당 | | | | |
| restaurant | | | | |

| 6 | 7 | 8 | 9 | 10 |
|---|---|---|---|---|
| waiter | chef | medium | tip | well-done |
| | | | | |

✎ 다음 단어의 우리말 뜻을 쓰고, 영어로 4번씩 반복해서 쓰세요.

| 1 | 2 | 3 | 4 | 5 |
| --- | --- | --- | --- | --- |
| post office | envelope | postcard | package | form |
| 우체국 | | | | |
| post office | | | | |

| 6 | 7 | 8 | 9 | 10 |
| --- | --- | --- | --- | --- |
| airmail | zip code | direct | regular | express |
| | | | | |

다음 단어의 우리말 뜻을 쓰고, 영어로 4번씩 반복해서 쓰세요.

| 1 | 2 | 3 | 4 | 5 |
|---|---|---|---|---|
| fire | call | help | thief | steal |
| 불, 화재 | | | | |
| fire | | | | |

| 6 | 7 | 8 | 9 | 10 |
|---|---|---|---|---|
| save | fire station | police office | firefighter | policeman |
| | | | | |

다음 단어의 우리말 뜻을 쓰고, 영어로 4번씩 반복해서 쓰세요.

| 1 | 2 | 3 | 4 | 5 |
|---|---|---|---|---|
| museum | visitor | palace | record | royal |
| 박물관 | | | | |
| museum | | | | |

| 6 | 7 | 8 | 9 | 10 |
|---|---|---|---|---|
| guidebook | thing | outstanding | treasure | exhibition |
| | | | | |

다음 단어의 우리말 뜻을 쓰고, 영어로 4번씩 반복해서 쓰세요.

| 1 | 2 | 3 | 4 | 5 |
|---|---|---|---|---|
| pain | sick | clinic | shot | hospital |
| 고통 | | | | |
| pain | | | | |

| 6 | 7 | 8 | 9 | 10 |
|---|---|---|---|---|
| patient | checkup | serious | flu | symptom |
| | | | | |

다음 단어의 우리말 뜻을 쓰고, 영어로 4번씩 반복해서 쓰세요.

| 1 | 2 | 3 | 4 | 5 |
|---|---|---|---|---|
| theater | movie | action | preview | horror |
| 극장 | | | | |
| theater | | | | |

| 6 | 7 | 8 | 9 | 10 |
|---|---|---|---|---|
| fantasy | mystery | trailer | interesting | festival |
| | | | | |

다음 단어의 우리말 뜻을 쓰고, 영어로 4번씩 반복해서 쓰세요.

| 1 | 2 | 3 | 4 | 5 |
|---|---|---|---|---|
| elect | agree | Congress | freedom | equality |
| 선출하다 | | | | |
| elect | | | | |

| 6 | 7 | 8 | 9 | 10 |
|---|---|---|---|---|
| lead | system | follow | politics | impeach |
| | | | | |

다음 단어의 우리말 뜻을 쓰고, 영어로 4번씩 반복해서 쓰세요.

| 1 | 2 | 3 | 4 | 5 |
|---|---|---|---|---|
| crime | law | lawyer | sentence | admit |
| 범죄 | | | | |
| crime | | | | |

| 6 | 7 | 8 | 9 | 10 |
|---|---|---|---|---|
| judge | situation | fact | court | prison |
| | | | | |

다음 단어의 우리말 뜻을 쓰고, 영어로 4번씩 반복해서 쓰세요.

| 1 | 2 | 3 | 4 | 5 |
|---|---|---|---|---|
| money | news | tax | account | economy |
| 돈 | | | | |
| money | | | | |

| 6 | 7 | 8 | 9 | 10 |
|---|---|---|---|---|
| property | boom | recovery | exchange | piggy bank |
| | | | | |

다음 단어의 우리말 뜻을 쓰고, 영어로 4번씩 반복해서 쓰세요.

| 1 | 2 | 3 | 4 | 5 |
|---|---|---|---|---|
| before | after | above | below | behind |
| 전에 | | | | |
| before | | | | |

| 6 | 7 | 8 | 9 | 10 |
|---|---|---|---|---|
| in front of | to | past | into | out of |
| | | | | |

✎ 다음 단어의 우리말 뜻을 쓰고, 영어로 4번씩 반복해서 쓰세요.

| 1 | 2 | 3 | 4 | 5 |
|---|---|---|---|---|
| inside | outside | top | bottom | accept |
| 안(쪽)에 | | | | |
| inside | | | | |

| 6 | 7 | 8 | 9 | 10 |
|---|---|---|---|---|
| reject | more | less | junior | senior |
| | | | | |

다음 단어의 우리말 뜻을 쓰고, 영어로 4번씩 반복해서 쓰세요.

| 1 | 2 | 3 | 4 | 5 |
|---|---|---|---|---|
| turn on | turn off | climb up | climb down | get on |
| 켜다 | | | | |
| turn on | | | | |

| 6 | 7 | 8 | 9 | 10 |
|---|---|---|---|---|
| get off | turn down | turn up | put on | take off |
| | | | | |

# Memo

# Memo

# Memo